# 101

# REAL ESTATE TIPS FOR BUYING A HOUSE

## THE ULTIMATE COLLECTION OF TIPS, TACTICS AND MORE FOR GETTING A GREAT DEAL

By

## Jeff Leighton

# Important Disclaimers

# Table of Contents

Important Disclaimers ............................................................3

Author's Note ....................................................................11

Introduction ....................................................................12

Section 1: Getting Started ........................................................13

   1. Should I Use A Real Estate Agent? ...........................13

   2. Should I Use My Friend Or Family Member Who Is An Agent? ...................................................................14

   3. What Are The Best Online Resources To Use When Buying A Home? .....................................................15

   4. How Do I Start The Home Search? Online Or In Person? ...............................................................16

   5. What Type Of Houses Should I Avoid? ......................17

   6. When Is The Best Time To Buy A House? ..................19

   7. What Are The Pros And Cons Of Buying A House? ...20

   8. Are Online Real Estate Sites Accurate? ....................21

   9. What Is The Standard Real Estate Commission? ......22

   10. Who Pays The Real Estate Agent Fees When Someone Buys A Home? ..........................................22

   11. What's The First Step In The Home-Buying Process? ...........................................23

Section 2: Building a Dream Team ..................................25

   12. How Do I Choose The Right Agent? .........................25

   13. Should I Sign An Exclusive Buyer's Agent Agreement? ...................................................26

14. What Is The Difference Between A Real
    Estate Agent And A Real Estate Broker? ...................27

15. How Do I Assemble An All-Star Real
    Estate Team? ..........................................................28

16. How Do I Know I Have Found The Right
    Real Estate Agent? ..................................................29

17. Should I Trust My Real Estate Agent? ......................31

Section 3: The Perfect House ..............................................33

18. How Do I Know What I Want To Buy?
    Should I Make A List? ..............................................33

19. How Should I Decide On Which Neighborhood
    I Want To Live In? ...................................................34

20. How Many Years Should I Plan To Stay
    In The Home? ..........................................................36

21. What Are HOA Fees? What Types Of
    Homes Have These? .................................................37

22. Should I Buy A House, Townhouse,
    Condo, Or Co-Op? ....................................................38

23. Is The School District Important? ...........................40

24. Should I Buy A Short Sale? ....................................40

25. Should I Buy A Foreclosure? ..................................42

26. How Long Does It Take To Buy A House? ...............43

27. The Pictures Look Bad. Should I Still See
    The House In Person? ..............................................44

28. What Are Off-Market Properties? ...........................45

29. How Many Houses Should I Look At
    Before Buying One? ................................................46

30. Do Condo Fees Ever Go Down? ..............................47

31. How Do I Know If I've Found
    The Perfect House? ................................................48

Section 4: Financing .........................................................50

32. How Much Should I Spend On A Home? ................50

33. How Do I Find The Best Lender With
The Best Terms? ........................................................51

34. What Are The Loan Application Steps? ...................52

35. How Much Of A Down Payment Will I Need? .........53

36. What Is PMI?............................................................53

37. What Is Seller Financing?........................................54

38. What Happens If My Loan Is Rejected? .................55

39. Should I Worry About Predatory Lenders? .............57

40. What Should I NOT Do Before Buying A House?....57

41. Should I Get A 15-Year Or A 30-Year Mortgage?.....58

42. What's The Difference Between Pre-Qualified
And Pre-Approved? ..................................................60

43. What If My House Does Not Appraise? ..................61

Section 5: House-Buying Tips ...........................................64

44. How Can I Find A Deal?...........................................64

45. Why Do People Always Talk About Location?.........65

46. Should I Buy A New Construction Home? ..............66

47. What Are The Pros And Cons Of Buying
A Fixer-Upper? ........................................................68

48. Should I Buy An Auction Property?.........................69

49. When Viewing Properties, What Should
I Look For?...............................................................71

50. What Time Of The Month Should I Close? .............73

51. What's The Deal With FSBOs? ................................74

52. How Much Should I Budget Once I Move In? .........75

53. Which Direction Is The Market Headed? ................76

54. Should I Buy A House With A Friend?.....................77

55. What Are Zestimates? Are They Accurate?.............79

56. Is The Market Overpriced? ......................................80

57. What Is The Commute Time?...................................81

58. Can I Get Rid Of Cigarette Smoke Or Other Smells?................................................82

59. Should I Buy In A Transitional Neighborhood?......83

60. How Do I Know If A Crime Was Committed In The House?..............................................86

61. Is The Neighborhood Safe? ....................................87

Section 6: Making Offers and Negotiating.........................88

62. What Is An Earnest Money Deposit (EMD)? ..........88

63. When Making An Offer, What Contingencies Should I Have?...................................89

64. How Do I Win In A Multiple-Offer Scenario?..........91

65. What Is A Seller Disclosure? ....................................93

66. What If The Seller Needs Time After Closing To Move? ......................................................95

67. What Happens If I Get Buyer's Remorse? ...............96

68. How Do I Cancel A Contract? ..................................98

69. Should I Send A Lowball Offer?...............................99

70. Can I Make Changes To The Contract After Going Under Contract?..................................100

71. Can I Write My Own Language Into The Contract?...........................................................101

72. What Is Negotiable In Real Estate?........................102

73. Is Price Per Square Foot Accurate? ........................102

74. What Questions Should I Ask Before Making An Offer? .....................................................103

75. How Long Does The Seller Have To Respond To Your Offer?.........................................104

76. How Does Real Estate Negotiation Work?.............105

77. How Much Should I Offer?.....................................106

Section 7: Inspections .......................................................108

78. Should I Get A Home Inspection? ..........................108

79. What Happens If The Inspection
Reveals Issues?..........................................................109

80. How Do I Make Sure Renovations Were
Done Correctly?........................................................111

81. Should I Get An Inspection On A New
Construction Home?................................................113

82. Should I Get A Radon Test?.....................................113

83. How Can I Find A Great Contractor? ......................114

84. Is The Crack A Foundational Crack Or
Just Cosmetic? .........................................................116

85. Should I Ask For Repairs Or A Credit?...................118

Section 8: The Final Steps of Closing the Deal.................120

86. How Do I Avoid Junk Fees? ....................................120

87. What Is A Loan Estimate?.......................................121

88. What Is A Closing Disclosure Form? ......................122

89. What Is A Home Warranty And Should
I Get One?.................................................................123

90. Should I Have A Real Estate Attorney
Look Over Documents? ...........................................125

91. How Does The Final Walk-Through Work?...........126

92. How Does Closing Work?.......................................128

93. What Will The Closing Costs Be? Who
Pays For Them?........................................................129

94. What Is A Title Search? ..........................................130

95. Should I Buy Owner's Title Insurance? ..................131

96. What Does Homeowners' Insurance Cover?..........133

Section 9: After You Buy ..................................................134

97. What Part Of Buying A Home Is
Tax Deductible?........................................................134

98. What Are The Biggest Expenses For First-Time
Home Buyers?..........................................................135

99. Which Home Improvements Can I Get
The Best Return On? ...............................................136

100. Is There Anything I Can Do
    To Eliminate Noise? ..................................................138

101. What Is The Cost Of Maintaining A House?.........139

Bonus 1: Ten Tips for Selling Your House ........................140

Bonus 2: House-Buying Hacks .........................................146

Bonus 3: Top Mistakes First-Time Home Buyers Make...153

Conclusion........................................................................160

About The Author............................................................162

# Author's Note

This book contains additional resources that I use on a daily basis as a real estate broker and real estate investor. Since I could not physically include these in the book, they are all available to download for free on my website www.jeff-leighton.com. That includes helpful videos, recommended resources, and much more.

# Introduction

Buying real estate is part of the American Dream. In this book, we will go over 101 things that you must know before buying your first property. Real estate can be one of the biggest wealth creators available and is also the largest investment of most people's lives. That is why the process should not be taken lightly, and you should be as informed as possible before buying a property.

In this book, I have handpicked the best ideas, strategies, and tips that every first-time home buyer must know when buying a property. Why should you listen to me? I am an active real estate broker and real estate investor with almost 10 years of experience, who has seen thousands of real estate deals, including the good, the bad, and the ugly. There is no theory in this book; it only contains practical, real-world tips and examples that you can use today. That being said, let's get into it.

# SECTION I

---

# Getting Started

## 1. Should I Use A Real Estate Agent?

Unless you are a professional real estate investor, I would highly recommend that you work with a real estate agent. Even the most mediocre real estate agent is better than you trying to buy a house yourself. I don't care how much HGTV you watch or how savvy you think you are, it's almost always a big mistake to buy without an agent.

The reason is that you need someone in your corner who is vouching for you. It is the listing agent's job to get as much money as possible for the seller in the most hassle-free way. That means that you, as a buyer, are on your own. You need an agent to help with you the price of the property, set your expectations, and work with you on contingencies and getting to closing.

Many buyers without agents are unaware of how the business works and can get frustrated. From my experience, it's usually the people that think they know everything and don't need an agent that are the most in need of help when buying a house. There are ways that I will go over in this guide to save money in any real estate transaction, but I would recommend not trying to save money this way.

## 2. Should I Use My Friend Or Family Member Who Is An Agent?

These days, everyone has a friend or a cousin who is a real estate agent. I would only recommend going with them if they are a full-time, highly rated agent. This is a huge financial decision, and mixing family and friendships with real estate can be a big risk, especially if they are not an established agent yet. If they have a successful track record, then I would say "maybe," but in my opinion, it's better to go with a local recommended agent who is not a friend or family member.

One thing in the deal that goes south can ruin your relationship; I've seen it happen numerous times. Keep in mind that anybody can get a real estate license, but there is a big difference between someone who just got licensed versus a savvy, experienced real estate agent.

## 3. What Are The Best Online Resources To Use When Buying A Home?

There are countless tools and websites that you can use to shop for a home. I would recommend as many as you feel comfortable with. Zillow, Redfin, Compass, and many other sites and apps can give you great information and make you a more informed consumer. Pinterest is another cool site where you can get great renovation and layout ideas for things like backyard landscaping, kitchens, living room ideas, and everything else in between.

In addition to browsing all the sites you can, I would even watch some of the HGTV or real estate shows out there. My favorite is *Million Dollar Listing*. While you might not be buying a million-dollar house, you will become more informed on how the real estate process works by watching these shows even though they are a little exaggerated. When buying a house, try to become just as informed as an agent would be. It will make your expectations and experience much smoother, and you can get a better deal by being more informed.

## 4. How Do I Start The Home Search? Online Or In Person?

I would start the process in both ways. Given the availability of information on different listings, you should start making yourself familiar with price ranges, styles of properties, and the average days on the market for different homes in your ideal locations.

In addition to that, I would recommend driving through various neighborhoods and attending open houses of all price ranges and styles. To really know what you want, you have to go out there and view properties in person. And you don't need a real estate agent to go see an open house; you can just walk in.

It happens all the time that a buyer thinks they want a particular neighborhood and a specific style of home only to realize once they start viewing these homes that they are looking for something entirely different. Photos can lie, so you need to get out there and view at least 25 properties of all price ranges in person in addition to your online research before you start narrowing in on exactly what you are looking for.

## 5. What Type Of Houses Should I Avoid?

In terms of livability and resale value, there are several types of properties I would avoid. The first type are houses on double yellow line roads, meaning that cars could come flying by, which gets old. I knew someone who had what they thought was the perfect house, even though it was on a double yellow line road. They ended up selling after a few years because of the speed and noise.

If you are in a big city and there's lots of people and activity, then that is different, but if you are in the suburbs, be careful about buying a property directly on a busy road. When you decide to resell the property, the number of buyers will be significantly limited.

Another thing you should avoid is buying properties directly in front of things like high schools, gas stations, power plants, or other potential things that could turn a buyer off. Sometimes buying in front of a school or right behind it is not an issue whatsoever, but if you are directly in front and have a ton of traffic, that will turn some people away.

When you are looking at resale value down the road, you want to have the largest pool of buyers available. If you buy directly in front of any of those, it will limit the pool of buyers. Now, if you just *have* to buy in front of one of these, then make sure there are comps from next door or very close by, because getting comps from just a block over could be significantly different than a comp facing the same way in front of those.

Lastly, I would avoid properties that are obsolete or not functional. In some older neighborhoods, you have houses that might only be 750 square feet and 2 bedrooms or other borderline tear-down houses. They will be priced significantly under the comps but in most cases, they have to be completely rebuilt right away or in the next few years. If you are a first-time home buyer, I would avoid these tear-down type properties because of the amount of work involved. When you go to sell it down the road, the only people interested are builders who are just buying the dirt and don't care what upgrades you might have done.

Whatever you do, make sure you don't buy a tear-down property on a double yellow line road in front of a school, gas station, or other eyesore!

## 6. When Is The Best Time To Buy A House?

There are a lot of theories out there on when is the best time of the year to buy a house. Some will say the winter time since there are fewer buyers, even though there are also fewer properties. In terms of price, the winter time generally speaking has the lowest median sold prices, but not by a lot, and there is also significantly less inventory.

A better strategy, in my opinion, is to be very clear on what you are looking for. When you do see something you like, make sure you act fast and put in an aggressive offer. An aggressive offer means having limited or no contingencies and offering full price or above asking price. Paying a little bit more for your dream home is better than trying to save a few bucks on a house in the winter time that you may or may not love.

## 7. What Are The Pros And Cons Of Buying A House?

Buying a house is a significant investment, and there are some pros and cons to consider when you buy your first property. We'll go over the cons first.

For starters, buying a property is a long-term decision, so if you think you might be moving soon, then I would not recommend buying a property. The only exception to that is if you can rent out the property to cover your mortgage.

Next, the repairs and renovations needed to maintain your house will probably be more expensive than you expect. If you do the right renovations, then your property could see appreciation, but you need to be prepared to fix an HVAC, roof, electrical, plumbing, and possibly other items.

Lastly, there is no guarantee that your property will increase in value. The longer you hold on to it, the more likely it will increase, but that's another reason to buy in a prime or up-and-coming area and stay close to the city if you want good resale value.

Some of the pros of buying a property include the tax benefits, e.g., the interest and property taxes that you can write off. There is also a sense of pride and accomplishment when buying a property. Lastly, real estate has made more millionaires than any other type of asset so, in my opinion, the earlier you start buying properties, the more you can start building appreciation.

## 8. Are Online Real Estate Sites Accurate?

When you're a first-time home buyer, I would highly recommend doing tons of online research about the local real estate market, neighborhood, prices, and more. However, that being said, the MLS or multiple listing service, which your agent will have you set up on is going to be your most accurate source of information for properties.

I can't tell you how many times I've gotten calls or emails about some hot new foreclosure property that is priced at some amazing deal on Zillow elsewhere. I'll look it up and the property either does not exist, or it's just bad information that was on the internet. Always verify with listings on the MLS. If you see something that does not seem right, check with your agent because it's not uncommon to have wrong information on some of these websites.

## 9. What Is The Standard Real Estate Commission?

The traditional real estate commission for residential real estate is 2.5% to 3% for the buyer's agent and 2.5% to 3% for the seller's agent. Now, technically speaking the commission can be any amount that is written into the listing agreement but 2.5% to 3% is standard across most markets.

## 10. Who Pays The Real Estate Agent Fees When Someone Buys A Home?

The seller always pays the real estate commission for both sides. That means, if you are a buyer, you do not have to factor in paying a 2.5%-3% commission to your agent. If you end up not buying a house, you don't owe anything either.

When a seller lists a property, they typically pay a 5% to 6% total commission, 3% to the buyer's agent and 3% to the seller's agent. Either way, the buyer doesn't pay any real estate agent fees. The only costs the buyer pays besides their down payment are home inspection fees, loan-related fees if you end up going under contract, and closing fees.

## 11. What's The First Step In The Home-Buying Process?

The first step of buying a house is getting preapproved from a local lender. I've seen many people who think they can afford a certain amount, when in reality it might be much lower – or much higher, for that matter. After you are pre-approved, you will know exactly what you can afford and can start looking for properties in those price ranges.

While searching for properties, make sure not to make any large purchases or switch jobs, since that can affect your ability to qualify for a loan. Lenders do not like to see changes in creditworthiness. Every now and then, the financing can get rejected if a buyer makes too large of a purchase or switches jobs a week before closing.

# SECTION 2

---

# Building a Dream Team

## 12. How Do I Choose The Right Agent?

There is no secret on how to find the right agent. I would recommend using these three strategies when looking for the right agent for you. Ask your friends, family members, and/or co-workers, and try to get a few names that come highly recommended. Everybody knows a good agent or two, and you can start building your list this way.

Next, you should look them up online on Zillow and other review sites to make sure they have good reviews and to see what other people are saying. Some agents might have 100 reviews, while others might only have one or two. This should help qualify your list a bit more. You can also drive around your target area and look up other agents that were not recommended but might have great reviews and be active in your neighborhood.

Finally, once you have several names, you should meet with at least two or three of them and interview them. If they all come recommended and all generally have good reviews, then chances are that they are all pretty good and would do a great job of helping you find your dream property. However, if you talk to two or three of them, chances are you will connect and get along with at least one out of the three, more so than the others. Then you have a winner.

Also, I would recommend finding an agent with a team. Many times, agents – like all of us – get busy. It's nice to have a transactional coordinator, buyer's agent, or another team member that can assist you on demand. Agents with teams are also generally more established and have more experience. Therefore, they can offer you better advice and insight.

## 13. Should I Sign An Exclusive Buyer's Agent Agreement?

There are two sides to this argument, and I have seen both of them. On the one hand, if you are an agent, you don't want to show someone 30 houses all weekend and then never hear from them again. Ask me how I know. On the other hand, if you are a buyer, you don't want to be stuck with one agent, especially if you are not sure they are the right fit for you.

I typically don't have buyers sign six-month agreements – or any agreements, for that matter – but I don't blame agents that do. On the other hand, please don't be the buyer that wants to see 30 houses and then never contacts the agent again. If you aren't sure whether you have found the right agent, a better strategy is to see a few properties or at least interview the agent before setting up hours of showings.

## 14. What Is The Difference Between A Real Estate Agent And A Real Estate Broker?

This is a pretty simple answer. A real estate agent is someone who has passed the required real estate exam and hangs their license with a brokerage. A real estate broker is someone who has their real estate licensed and has taken additional courses and required experience to pass their broker's test and now has a broker's license.

Most states require that a broker work for at least three years as an active agent and have done a certain number of deals in addition to further coursework. In other words, the majority of real estate professionals are not real estate brokers. The main difference is that a broker can own their own brokerage and employ agents under them, while an agent has to work under a broker.

## 15. How Do I Assemble An All-Star Real Estate Team?

To build your all-star real estate team of a real estate agent, lender, title company, home inspector, and contractors, there are really only a couple of ways. Keep in mind as well that when you are building your team, you should think about getting several names for each type of professional instead of relying on one. Each professional will offer different value propositions and have a slightly different way of doing business.

The first way to start building your list of real estate professionals is from referrals. Ask your co-workers, friends, family, or anyone that has recently bought a house if they had a great experience. Some people you talk to will have had an amazing experience while others maybe not so much. After building your list of referrals, start doing some online research for top-rated real estate agents, inspectors, title companies, and lenders.

Ideally, some of the same names that came highly recommended to you should also be on the highest-rated lists when you do your online search.

Since real estate is such a high-stakes business, I would stay away from using a friend or family member who might offer a discount, unless of course, they are a top-rated professional with a lot of experience.

## 16. How Do I Know I Have Found The Right Real Estate Agent?

To begin with, you should only use real estate agents who come highly recommended and have great online reviews. After that, your agent should have the following traits.

**Local knowledge**. They should be able to offer you insight based on their experience in this exact neighborhood or building. If they are coming from 45 minutes away, they probably do not have local knowledge, and you should probably find a more local expert.

Next, they should be **responsive**. That doesn't mean they need to respond to text messages or calls at every hour of the night, but they should respond to you in a reasonable time, at least within an hour. Since sometimes you might need to see a property ASAP, it is crucial that you have a responsive agent.

**Professional**. This can be a subjective trait, but I prefer to work with agents that are well dressed, speak knowledgeably, and maybe even have a nice car. I know that is kind of a real estate agent stereotype, but I wouldn't want my agent showing up in a beater car full of junk, wearing a T-shirt and drinking a smoothie, which I have seen before.

**Tech-savvy.** You need to have an agent that is tech-savvy. If your agent wants to fax contracts to you or always meet in person to sign documents, this is a warning sign. The real estate business moves too fast to operate like you are in the 1970s. You can digitally sign offers these days, so avoid agents that are too old-school.

Lastly, your agent should have a **positive attitude and be easy to work with**. Some agents that you work with give you the feeling you could hang out with them all day, while other agents make you absolutely dread the idea of even talking to them. Some agents will make business unnecessarily complicated or have a very difficult personality. There's no reason to work with someone like that. You need to make sure your agent is friendly and easy to get along with. Most are, but just keep this in mind.

## 17. Should I Trust My Real Estate Agent?

Real estate agents, like many salespeople, have gotten a bad reputation over the years, but I think it's mostly exaggerated. Keep in mind that for a real estate agent to stay in business and be successful, it means they have to give you, the customer, a fantastic experience with the hope that you refer them to as many people as possible. Even though you may see real estate agent open house signs and real estate agents posting on Facebook about their newest listing, most agents do not get any deals from their marketing. They rely almost entirely on building a huge referral network.

Real estate agents become successful by giving their sellers and buyers an amazing experience that the clients tell everyone about. That being said, make sure you find a real estate agent who comes highly recommended, has excellent reviews, and does business in the area you are looking at. I would trust your agent; but at the same time, I would also be an educated consumer and try to learn about the neighborhoods, prices, and anything else before making any offers.

# SECTION 3

---

# The Perfect House

## 18. How Do I Know What I Want To Buy? Should I Make A List?

You will know what you want to buy by initially starting your search online and making a list of some things you are looking for. However, and I can't emphasize this enough, once you start viewing places in person, your list will change, so keep an open mind to different homes. That is why, before you seriously start looking at properties to make an offer, you should visit all different styles, price ranges, and neighborhoods to really see what you are looking for. You can even stay at an Airbnb of different types of properties to see what it's like.

Also, the photos will lie. Most of the time, the property will look much nicer in the pictures than in person, although sometimes it's the other way around. Go to as many open houses as possible before seriously considering homes with your agent.

## 19. How Should I Decide On Which Neighborhood I Want To Live In?

When deciding where you want to live, I like to keep four things in mind: your ideal lifestyle, proximity to friends and family, resale value, and – everybody's favorite – commute time.

As far as lifestyle goes, do you prefer to be within walking distance of all the restaurants, bars, and city life, or are you more of a country person who wants a couple of acres and doesn't want to be right on top of your neighbors? Depending on your age and interests, this will help clarify what neighborhood is best.

Also, keep in mind your proximity to friends and family. If this is a big factor for you, which it is for most people, then moving 30 or 45 minutes away is a big hurdle. I know that does not seem like very long, but I can tell you from first-hand experience, once somebody moves over 30 minutes away, it becomes significantly more difficult to visit each other.

Next, resale value is the most critical factor for some people. If that's the case, I would recommend moving into a smaller property, maybe even a fixer-upper, in a transitional neighborhood where a lot of development is going on. I don't know who said it, but when it comes to resale value, "it's better to buy a shithole in the up-and-coming neighborhood than a castle in no-where's-land."

I've seen sellers who have owned a property for over 10 years not see any appreciation in a beautiful house in the suburbs far outside the city, where commutes average an hour each way. At the same time, I've seen other sellers who moved into the up-and-coming neighborhood and bought an absolute fixer-upper, double or even triple the price they originally paid in just a few years.

Lastly, when figuring out where to live, keep in mind where your job is located. If you work from home, great, but if not, make sure you drive or test the commute times before making a purchase.

Overall, you should keep those four factors in mind and also do a ton of research online about the different neighborhoods and what people are saying. Nowadays, you can even Airbnb for a couple days or week in these different neighborhoods to see which one you like the best.

## 20. How Many Years Should I Plan To Stay In The Home?

If you do research online, you will find that the average home buyer lives in their property for an average of anywhere from three to ten years, and even one estimate at thirteen years before they move. That being said, I think you should plan on living in your property for at least five years so that you can build up equity and possibly even see an increase in value.

If you hold on to your property for at least seven years, there is a very good chance of appreciation according to the real estate market cycles. If you move before three years, you might have to come out of pocket at the closing table because of the commissions, closing costs, and transaction fees.

## 21. What Are HOA Fees? What Types Of Homes Have These?

HOA or homeowner association fees are common in some single-family home and townhome communities. They vary from community to community and typically go towards things like trash removal, insurance of common areas, lawn care, and sometimes amenities like pools, playgrounds, security, and more. The fees can vary from as little as $100 per year upwards to $1,000 per month. According to the Foundation for Community Research Association, about 25% of Americans live in a neighborhood that has an HOA.

A homeowner association has rules and regulations for the community for things such as exterior paint colors, the size of pets, trees, architectural restrictions, and more. Some HOAs are stricter than others, although generally speaking, most homeowners have a favorable impression of their HOA because the community maintains a professional look, which could, in turn, help property values.

Always look up your HOA online to find out any additional information and be sure to ask the seller how strict they are if you have any questions. Standard real estate contracts will allow you a period of usually three days to review the HOA docs and cancel your contract for any reason if you don't like something in the docs. If you are worried about the fees, then look up the previous several years of fees to see how much they have increased. These fees do not tend to go up anywhere near as much as condo fees.

## 22. Should I Buy A House, Townhouse, Condo, Or Co-Op?

What type of property you buy is a lifestyle choice you need to make. If you have a large family, then a single-family house is probably best, but if you are a bachelor, then maybe living in a condo with a nice view in the downtown part of the city is better. If you are thinking in terms of appreciation, countless studies have been done. Generally speaking, they say that single-family homes tend to appreciate more than townhomes and that townhomes tend to appreciate more than condos.

That being said, I think the location is still the determining factor when it comes to appreciation. For example, if I had bought the smallest studio condo in the transitional part of town five years ago versus buying a nice single-family house 30 minutes outside of the city in the suburbs, then the studio condo would have appreciated more – and it's not even close. If you are really looking for appreciation, then buy a single-family house in an up-and-coming neighborhood close to the core of the city.

However, buying a property is not always about buying the one with the most potential appreciation. Lifestyle is the other factor. Always be sure to drive around in the neighborhood and get a good understanding of how far you are away from the city, from your job, friends, and more. I had a friend move out to the suburbs about 40 minutes away from me, and now I hardly see them anymore because of the distance. Just something to keep in mind. You need to weigh those three factors, appreciation, lifestyle, and distance from friends, family, and activities.

## 23. Is The School District Important?

Even if you don't have kids, you should keep in mind how good of a school district you are purchasing in. Just one block down the street could be an entirely different school district with a much higher rating. For some buyers, the school district is the number one factor in their decision. That means they would move into a mediocre house as long as it's in an amazing school district.

Now, if you are considering moving into a transitional neighborhood with a lot of development going on, you could expect that the school district would get better year over year. In terms of resale value, being in a good school district is something that should play a factor in your purchase, but I don't think it should be a deal breaker if you don't have kids in school or plan on kids in the next five years or so.

## 24. Should I Buy A Short Sale?

Short sales can offer an excellent opportunity for a savvy home buyer, but they can come with additional issues. Short sales are properties where the owner owes much more than the house is worth, is experiencing a hardship of some sort, and needs to sell. The bank typically prefers to do a short sale than a foreclosure because the process is less expensive for them.

When you buy a short sale, you can make any offer you want. The listing price set by the agent is usually a lot lower than the comps so that they can get an offer quickly, although you can still feel free to offer lower. With short sales, you need to be patient; it can easily take six months. In some scenarios, if you are lucky, a short sale can take just a month or two, and in more extreme cases, I have seen short sales take over a year.

There is also no guarantee that the short sale will go through. You can be under contract with the seller for months on end at a given price, but the bank still needs to approve the price and get to closing. I've seen buyers who have given up on the deal after several months. Another thing to note about short sales is that while you can do a home inspection, the seller and/or bank won't do any repairs, so you are buying the house as is.

That being said, if you are okay buying a fixer-upper property and patient enough to wait out the process, a short sale can be a great opportunity to purchase discounted real estate. If you look at the comps in every neighborhood, the lowest-priced houses by far are usually the short sales. There is less competition with short sales and, unlike a foreclosure, the seller is still living there so, theoretically, the house should still be in livable condition.

## 25. Should I Buy A Foreclosure?

A foreclosure is where the property is owned by the bank. These are vacant homes that need work. Every now and then, a foreclosure is in excellent condition, but generally speaking, you should expect the property to need work. With foreclosures, you can do a home inspection, but the bank does not usually offer a credit or do repairs. Foreclosures are typically priced towards the lower end of the comps, although you need to make sure the repair costs justify the lower price. Sometimes, foreclosures are overpriced, just like any other property.

If you do decide to buy a foreclosure, make sure your lender is aware because they will have certain property requirements, such as having appliances, no leaking roof, and other things like that. Overall, a traditional lender will want a "livable" property if they are making a loan on it. When buying a foreclosure, make sure no one is living there, which sometimes happens with squatters.

Also, don't be afraid to offer a lower amount than the offer price. Even if it's already one of the lowest comps, it doesn't hurt to try a lower offer. The bank will usually respond within a few days or a week, but it will be nowhere near as long as a short sale, so you should hear back soon.

For a savvy home buyer who doesn't mind doing a little bit of work, a foreclosure can be a great purchase. And while most people think that foreclosures are only in the worst neighborhoods, you can find them in nearly every type of area.

## 26. How Long Does It Take To Buy A House?

Once you get a property under contract, the

standard closing period is 30 days. That being said, the timeframe for buying a house is usually much longer than that because of the preparation for getting a preapproval, looking at properties, and possibly making a couple of offers before one gets accepted. Some buyers take as little as 30 days to buy a house, while others search for the perfect home for over a year. I would say, on average, once you start seriously looking at properties, it should not take more than three to six months.

If you are in a competitive market, it is not uncommon to have multiple offers on properties you are looking at, so you have to make several offers before getting one accepted. In less competitive markets, your first offer could be accepted – I see it happen all the time.

## 27. The Pictures Look Bad. Should I Still See The House In Person?

If a property meets most of your requirements and is in the perfect neighborhood but the photos look bad, I would not let that discourage you from seeing the property. I can't tell you how many times I've been to houses that look much better in person than online. Many times, you have to actually go to the property to get a full idea of the home. The opposite is true as well, if you have a fantastic photographer, they can make even the most drab-looking house look like the Taj Mahal.

It is slightly annoying when I see agents upload awful photos of a property because it makes our industry look lazy and makes the house look bad. That being said, bad photos can be a huge opportunity for you because many buyers will overlook the house. As a result, you could get a better deal since there will be less competition.

If you look at the history of Airbnb, the whole reason they attribute to the skyrocketing of their popularity is getting professional photography done for their listings. When they initially had properties listed, many of the photos were dark, uninviting, and unprofessional. Nowadays, they will send a professional Airbnb photographer for free to take pictures for your listing so that they can present it in the best possible light.

## 28. What Are Off-Market Properties?

Off-market properties are homes that were never listed but were sold anyway. Believe it or not, about 10% of properties that are sold never hit the market. Most of the time, it is investors that market to motivated sellers and are looking for people that need to sell fast. However, if you are savvy and know of estate sales, pre-foreclosures, or anyone else in the neighborhood looking to sell fast, you can approach them with an offer. Off-market properties typically come with a discount because the seller is looking to sell quickly and without any hassle.

## 29. How Many Houses Should I Look At Before Buying One?

Before I give you the number, I would recommend doing a ton of online research and going to open houses of all price ranges and styles before seriously considering buying a home. I have seen many instances where someone had their mind set on a townhouse only to end up with a single-family house or even a condo after viewing the properties in person.

In real estate investing, we always talk about the rule of 100, where you should look at 100 deals before choosing one. When it comes to buying a house to live in, I think you need to view an absolute minimum of 10 homes if you already know what you are looking for. Ideally, you should look at about 25-30 houses. You can do a lot of this without an agent since you could probably see at least 10 homes every weekend before you start your serious search.

## 30. Do Condo Fees Ever Go Down?

I have never heard of condo fees going down. I am sure that if you really looked hard, you could find a couple examples here and there of small condo buildings where the fees have gone down over the years, but I have never heard of that. The fees trend upwards, although that does not mean you can't still get a good deal.

The condo fees go towards maintaining interior areas like hallways, a fitness center, exterior maintenance like landscaping, snow removal, walls and fences, security for the building, insurance, reserve funds, and sometimes utilities as well. If you lived in a single-family house, you would still have many of these expenses; you just would not pay a monthly fee for them.

One of the best ways to get an idea of the condo fees is to have your real estate agent look up the average condo fee over the last five years. I actually just did this for a client and it gave us a great idea of where the fees might be in the future.

Most of the time, what you will see is a consistent trend upwards of prices, though it's not usually a dramatic increase. The general rule of thumb is that older condo buildings have higher fees because they need more maintenance. Luxury buildings with lots of amenities also tend to see higher increases in fees.

## 31. How Do I Know If I've Found The Perfect House?

When you have found the right house, you should have a feeling of excitement. The way it usually works is the property will show up online on one of your searches and will meet just about all the criteria you are looking for. You will immediately contact your agent to see it ASAP. Sometimes the property is what you think it is; sometimes it's worse; sometimes it's better.

However, once you see it in person and you know the comps and the neighborhood, and you are still excited about the property, you should put in an aggressive offer as soon as you can. I see too often that buyers find something that is pretty good but not exactly what they are looking for.

They usually end up backing out of the deal during a contingency period or, in some cases, buying a house they are not entirely sold on. Make sure you are excited about your purchase. And not only that, but you should have already looked at 20, 30, or even 50 houses in person so that you know exactly when you have found "the one."

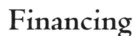

# Financing

## 32. How Much Should I Spend On A Home?

The first step in the home-buying process is to get pre-approved so that you know how much you can afford. A loan officer will take a look at your income, assets, liabilities, credit, and other factors and give you a price point that you can reasonably afford. Now, keep in mind that just because you get approved for 500K does not mean you need to spend that much.

Your monthly payment should not be a stretch. If you are not able to save money every month after paying your monthly mortgage, then I would recommend buying a lower-priced house. Or, if you are purchasing a property at the top of your budget, I would recommend renting out the basement or a room or two to a friend. The biggest thing I can tell you about buying houses is to always have a three- to six-month cash cushion available for unexpected expenses and for peace of mind.

## 33. How Do I Find The Best Lender With The Best Terms?

When looking for a good lender, I would try to find at least three local highly recommended lenders. You can start your search by asking your real estate agent, friends, family, or anyone else that recently had a good experience. Additionally, you can look up all the references online and see who has the best reviews. I would recommend a local lender instead of a large national company with a 1-800 number that goes to a call center in Florida or elsewhere for a couple of reasons.

Local lenders with an available cell phone, email, and good reputation make your offer look much stronger than if you use a large corporation with a 1-800 number. Not only that, but local lenders tend to have a better track record of closing on time and without headache. Within a few days of going under contract, you should choose which lender is best, lock in your rate, and get all the financing going.

## 34. What Are The Loan Application Steps?

To apply for a mortgage, you will need recent pay stubs, bank statements, tax returns, monthly expenses, and a credit score check. You can email those over to a mortgage broker or meet one in person and give them the information. I would recommend filling out a couple of applications to see who has the best rates and options for you. It should be free to apply for the loan, although they might charge you for a credit check. Once you review the loan estimates, you can choose one and lock in your rate.

Throughout the home-buying process, you should be in constant contact with your lender to make sure they have everything they need and that you are still on track for closing. Some of the mortgage-related fees include the appraisal fee, loan origination fee, points, mortgage broker fee, and other related fees. That's why it's important to get at least three estimates, so you know all the costs and can make the best pick. Your lender also has to give you a loan estimate which goes over your interest rate, monthly payment, and total closing costs for a loan.

## 35. How Much Of A Down Payment Will I Need?

There are countless loan programs out there, and many involve less than 20% down. While 20 percent is the traditional amount people put down, there are plenty of loan options for as little as 3.5%, 5%, 10%, and even 0% down if you are a veteran. Many first-time home buyers opt for the FHA 3.5% down payment so that they can have some funds available for renovations or reserve funds. Before deciding on any loan, you should reach out to several local highly recommended lenders and see what loan products they have, what their rates are, and any other fees.

## 36. What Is PMI?

PMI or private mortgage insurance is a type of mortgage insurance that lenders usually require if you are putting a down payment of less than 20%. The PMI protects the lender in case you stop making payments and is a fee that is added to your monthly mortgage. According to Trulia, the cost of PMI on an annual basis is usually about .2 to 1.5 percent of your loan. For example, if you financed 100% of a 200K property, your PMI fee using the .2 to 1.5 percent number would be somewhere between $33 to $250 per month.

The good thing is that once you have built up 20% equity in the property, your PMI will be canceled. Always contact your lender about PMI questions because there are many variables and the rules on PMI are always changing. While PMI may seem like a burden, it is also nice to be able to finance a property without having to put 20% down. You could save some cash up front by doing a 3.5%, 5%, or 10% loan instead of 20%.

## 37. What Is Seller Financing?

Seller financing is exactly what it sounds like. It is available on a very small percentage of properties out there. While it's certainly not the norm, some sellers will advertise the property as being open to seller financing, where the seller is essentially the bank. Most MLS services will have a way to sort by properties that are open to seller financing. You would sign a promissory note with the seller that shows the interest rate, repayment schedule, and the default consequences.

It is not very common, but a seller would offer seller financing to try to get their property sold faster, open it up to more potential buyers, and make a nice interest off of the note. For buyers, seller financing can offer a way to buy a property with fewer closing costs and fees involved since there are no banks. You can also typically close faster and won't need to get the approval of a traditional lender. Since seller financing is not as common as traditional bank financing, make sure you do research and talk to a lawyer and real estate agent before signing on that type of deal.

## 38. What Happens If My Loan Is Rejected?

When making an offer, it is standard to include a financing contingency. That means that if your financing gets rejected and the financing contingency is in place, you will be able to withdraw your offer without penalty and get your earnest money deposit back. That being said, it is unusual to get your financing rejected unless your lender never verified your tax and income documents, or in the event of job loss or significant change in your creditworthiness.

When making an offer, you should be in constant contact with your lender and be sure not to make any large purchases, change jobs, accept large monetary gifts, or have too many credit inquiries.

Sometimes your loan might be rejected because of a low appraisal. If you do get a low appraisal, then you have the option to go back to the seller and request that they lower the price to the appraised value so that your loan will go through. Most sellers, except in egregious cases of a low appraisal, will work with you to lower their price to the appraised value.

They typically don't want to risk putting the property on the market again and then going through the process again only to get another low appraisal. If you have waived your financing contingency, which is common in multiple-offer scenarios, you have to be 100% sure your financing will go through. In the unlikely event your financing gets rejected, your earnest money deposit could be put at risk.

## 39. Should I Worry About Predatory Lenders?

I would not worry too much about predatory lenders. The market crash of 2007 wiped out a lot of the bad elements of real estate and forced the industry to make significant regulatory changes. Nowadays, getting a loan is a much stricter process and there are fewer bad apples out there, in my opinion. When looking for a lender, I would always do your research online and through recommendations from your real estate agent and friends. Once you have found three recommended lenders, check to see who has the best rates and service, and go with one of them.

## 40. What Should I NOT Do Before Buying A House?

Once you are approved for buying a house and get under contract, there are a couple of things that can completely sabotage your deal and that you need to avoid at all costs. For starters, do not make any large purchases whatsoever, including furniture, cars, or any other substantial purchase that could affect your buying power.

Secondly, do not change jobs. Even if you are moving on to a bigger and better job, wait until after your purchase to change jobs. Most purchase contracts have a 30-day closing period, so you should be able to work it out.

Next, make sure there are no more inquiries into your credit. This goes hand in hand with making large purchases, but be aware that the more inquiries you have, the lower your credit score will go, which can ultimately affect your ability to get qualified for your loan.

Next, make sure you put utilities into your name effective for the day of settlement.

Lastly, make sure you have a good line of communication between your lender, the title company, and your agent. Make sure your lender has everything they need from you and check in with your title company and agent at least once a week to make sure everything is on track for closing.

## 41. Should I Get A 15-Year Or A 30-Year Mortgage?

Let's evaluate the pros and cons of a 15-year vs. a

30-year mortgage. To begin with, if you are going with a 15-year loan, your mortgage payment will be higher because the loan is consolidated into only 15 years. However, your interest rate will be much better than for a 30-year loan. Lenders see less risk with a 15-year loan and, as a result, they will give you a better interest rate. You need to be sure that you can comfortably pay the higher monthly payment while still having money left over for reserves and unexpected expenses. Do not stretch yourself too thin because with house buying there are always unexpected costs, and life events can change your financial situation.

With a 15-year loan, you will also qualify for a less expensive property than if you were to go with a traditional 30-year term. Also, since you are paying off the property faster, you will have a smaller mortgage interest deduction on your taxes.

With a 30-year mortgage, you will be able to build up more savings and additional funds since you are not putting as much towards a house payment every month. Some experts recommend a 15-year mortgage, though, because it's a forced savings plan and can help you build equity fast.

You should know that even if you get a 30-year mortgage, you can still make extra payments and pay it off in 15 years if you choose to.

Overall, when deciding on a loan product, make sure to do your research and evaluate all options before locking in. Both 15- and 30-year loans can work great, but every situation is different.

## 42. What's The Difference Between Pre-Qualified And Pre-Approved?

The first step for buying a property is getting prequalified or preapproved. Some lenders use these interchangeably, but there are some differences to be aware of. Most of the time, when you are prequalified with a lender, it means you have submitted your financial information, including income, debts, credit score, and assets to your lender. They will then issue you a prequalification form. Many lenders can do this quickly, even within minutes. However, while it may be correct, a prequalification does not check your actual documents, such as bank statements, pay stubs, tax returns, and other info.

For your own sake, so you know how much you can afford and to give the seller more comfort that you are a strong buyer, you should get a preapproval letter, where your lender will verify your documents. Too many people have abused the system and just get printed out prequalification forms online that take two minutes to obtain. Get a strong preapproval letter. When you submit your offer, you can even recommend that your lender calls the listing agent to let them know that you are a slam dunk buyer.

## 43. What If My House Does Not Appraise?

Every now and then, a property you purchase might not appraise. That means the independent appraiser has to verify that the property is worth at least as much as you are paying for it. They don't want the bank making loans on overvalued properties. If you have an appraisal contingency in your offer, which is standard, you can go back to the seller and request that they lower the price to the appraised amount.

If the seller refuses, then you have the option to either come up with the extra cash needed in the difference of the appraisal amount or cancel the contract without penalty (i.e., losing your earnest money deposit). In most cases, if a property does not appraise, the seller lowers their price to the appraised amount, although sometimes they will request that you meet in the middle.

Every now and then, they will challenge the appraisal if it appears that their appraisal report made egregious mistakes. Sometimes sellers will simply refuse to budge on the price, relist their property on the market, and hope that any other offers with a new lender and new appraiser will have the property appraise.

Generally speaking, it is unusual for a property to appraise more or less than the sales price you have it under contract. Usually, it appraises right at the price you have it at because, as I said, the bank wants to make sure it's worth at least what you are paying for it; it's not an exact science.

In a competitive situation with multiple offers, it can be an excellent strategy to waive the appraisal contingency. In the worst-case scenario, you would have to come out of pocket to cover any difference in the appraisal. However, as I mentioned, properties usually appraise except in very extreme situations.

# SECTION 5

◆━━◆━━◆

# House-Buying Tips

## 44. How Can I Find A Deal?

The best advice I can give you on this is to be educated. Savvy real estate investors have something called the rule of 100, where they like to evaluate 100 potential deals before buying one. You should use a similar strategy for your house hunting by looking online and even going to open houses or driving by different homes that are in the ballpark of your criteria.

When you are new to real estate, you won't always know what makes a great deal or a bad deal. You need to educate yourself on the market from online research, in-person open houses, driving around in neighborhoods, and talking to people you know who have recently bought a home.

## 45. Why Do People Always Talk About Location?

You may have heard the term "location, location, location," but what does that actually mean? It means that no matter what type of house it is, no matter the condition of the house, the location is the most significant factor in the value of the property. The property will go up or down in value because of the location above all else.

Some of the considerations that go into location, location, location include good school districts, transportation options including walkability, proximity to downtown and entertainment, shops, restaurants, and more.

Everybody knows this principle when getting into real estate. I remember one specific story that always stuck with me. A couple bought a near-million-dollar home in a brand new planned community about 45 minutes outside of the city. Ten years later, they still can't sell their house, even at a significant six figure loss.

Their property value is now worth roughly the same as a dilapidated house in a booming up-and-coming part of the city that was bought at the same time. The moral of the story is that if you want to buy the perfect house with the perfectly manicured lawn in the middle of nowhere, then you must be prepared for your value to stay the same or even drop.

If you are looking for resale value, then you must buy in an up-and-coming or established "blue chip" area that is close to everything. Nobody wants to have to commute an hour each way, no matter how beautiful the house is. In terms of resale value, people would rather be able to walk to restaurants, the nightlife, and live in a smaller fixer-upper house than live in a palace in the middle of nowhere.

## 46. Should I Buy A New Construction Home?

There are a couple of benefits to buying a new home. For starters, depending on when you make an offer on the property, you will be able to customize it quite a bit. Additionally, with new homes, there is much less maintenance, and you won't have to worry about replacing the HVAC or roof anytime soon. Your house will also typically have some excellent amenities in the community, such as a pool, park, or close proximity to transit. Most builders are doing that nowadays.

On the other side of the equation, most new construction, while it could be close to transit, is still a ways away from the city. You would need to factor in commute times as well as proximity to friends and family.

Price is another thing to keep in mind. In many new construction developments, the price is the price, and it's not as flexible as an older property. You will be paying a premium for new construction properties. When looking at buying new construction, unless you know you have a great deal, you should wait for a few new construction comps in that neighborhood to sell first so you know the value of what others have paid. I have seen it happen too many times that the first buyer into a new community or development pays the highest price.

Lastly, if you are into neighborhood character, there might not be a ton of that in a new development. Everything is brand new and looks similar. I prefer historic properties that have unique features, but those come with a lot of maintenance, unlike new construction, and are usually smaller and less efficient. Overall, you need to think about what is most important to you and talk to people that have lived or live in both types of properties.

## 47. What Are The Pros And Cons Of Buying A Fixer-Upper?

If you are comfortable doing repairs and come from a construction background, a fixer-upper property can be a great option. However, if you are completely new to real estate, then I would give you some words of caution with fixer-uppers. The biggest mistake I see newer real estate buyers and investors make is underestimating repair costs. A 30K renovation can quickly become a 75K renovation project if you don't have a lot of experience.

I have done numerous renovation projects, and I can tell you from first-hand experience that they can take a lot longer than expected. If you are living in the house while the renovations are being done, it can get stressful for you and your significant other.

That being said, one of the best parts about buying a fixer-upper is that you are purchasing the lowest-priced house in the neighborhood. And just because you see a house that needs work listed on the market does not mean it's a good deal. It also needs to be at or near the lowest of the prices in the area. Sometimes fixer-uppers are way overpriced given the amount of repairs needed.

A great thing about fixer-uppers is how rewarding they can be when you customize your own house to your design. Taking an older home and giving it a new fresh look is a great feeling. What's even better is the improvement in value that you should see when you sell it. So overall, if you want to get a great deal, don't mind getting your hands dirty, and want to see some equity at the end of it, then a fixer-upper can be a great option.

## 48. Should I Buy An Auction Property?

Auctions are fascinating to go to, but unless you

are an experienced real estate investor with cash, I would not go there to buy property – apart from a few exceptions which I will go over. When you go to an auction, the property has to meet a minimum amount set by the bank, which you don't find out until you get to the auction. The majority of the time, the property goes back to the bank because it does not meet the minimum bid and then you will see the property show up many months down the road listed on the market as an REO or foreclosure.

With auctions, you are almost never allowed to view the inside of the house, so you have to be comfortable with estimating repairs from only viewing the exterior. In addition to that, if your bid gets accepted, you have to put down a large cash deposit and you will have a hard time using any type of traditional financing for the deal. There also might still be people living in there that you have to evict or pay cash for keys to get them to leave.

Now, I know I'm not painting a great picture of auctions, but there are a few instances where I think buying an auction property could work. If the property is a condo in a building you are familiar with, then there is a lot less risk. Even if the entire inside needs to be gutted, which is highly unlikely, it's still just a condo. If you know the property because it's in your neighborhood or maybe you even knew someone that lived in it, then that could be some valuable info that allows you to make a more informed offer.

In areas like Arizona, Michigan, Maryland, and other states with tens of thousands of foreclosures, investors use bidding services, whom they tell exactly what their maximum price is for a property. Then the buyer only has to pay if they get the deal at their ideal price and the buyer does not actually have to physically be there at every auction. If you have a competitive advantage like that or some type of additional information that can give you an advantage, then auctions could be a good idea.

However, generally speaking, I think auctions are fascinating to watch, but I would not recommend buying an auction property, especially if you are a first-time home buyer.

## 49. When Viewing Properties, What Should I Look For?

When viewing properties, there are several things you need to be aware of. The first is, how busy is the street? Living on a double yellow line road or busy area can get old pretty quickly. I knew someone who had to back out of his driveway every day, where cars were flying by at almost 50 miles per hour.

Next, I would check the neighborhood by driving or walking around. What kind of street is it? What do the houses look like? How close are you to different amenities? Walk around the neighborhood, even at night, to make sure you would feel comfortable living there.

Next, get an overall feel for the property. Does it seem like there's a lot of deferred maintenance or has the seller done a lot of upgrades? If it looks like the seller took some shortcuts on things you can see, then chances are they probably also took shortcuts on other items that are not entirely visible. Always get a good home inspection and keep a reserve fund for repairs to your property.

Next, if there is a basement, try to note if there is any musty smell or how the grading and landscaping is in the back. Basement water issues are no joke. A better way of avoiding water issues if you are concerned is just to buy a house without a basement or with a walk-out basement.

Keep in mind that every basement, especially if it's an older house, has a "basement smell," so I would only be concerned if it's a really moldy smell and there is evidence of water damage. Nowadays, though, even if you end up buying a house with water issues, there are countless ways of fixing the problem. Waterproofing basements is a big business, and there are numerous ways to waterproof a basement that are very affordable.

So overall, check out how busy the street is, what kind of neighborhood it is, the overall condition of the property, and the basement.

## 50. What Time Of The Month Should I Close?

Many home buyers want to close at the end of the month and believe that it's the best time to settle. The reason is, when you buy a property, your interest will start accruing on the day you close. If you close on the first of the month, you will have to pay the closing cost interest from your closing date until the end of that month. If you had closed towards the end of the month, you would only be paying interest for a couple of days as opposed to a couple of weeks or so if you closed early or mid-month. Many people prefer to have a little bit more cash in hand when they close, so that's why they choose the end of the month.

There are no real savings since you will be paying the same amount one way or another, but you will have slightly more cash in hand if you closed towards the end of the month. Since it gets so busy towards the end of the month, with people thinking they are saving money, I would choose to close early in the month or mid-month, when it's not as hectic at the title company.

## 51. What's The Deal With FSBOs?

I have a pretty strong opinion on FSBOs (for sale by owner), given that I used to list them for a couple of hundred bucks on the MLS when I was getting started as an agent. The only reason I listed them was that my real estate broker told me I could then tell people the next year that I sold tens of millions of dollars worth of properties and basically trick them into thinking I was a top broker. When you list a property as an FSBO as a flat-fee service, all you are doing is submitting it to the MLS; you are not doing any negotiation or anything.

But anyways, I found FSBOs to be some of the most unmotivated sellers out there, and they are usually priced a good amount higher than the comps. It would blow my mind how unrealistic many of these sellers are. However, that being said, just like any niche, there are probably ways you can master it and get good deals.

Maybe, if you know someone local who is considering listing their property, you can talk to them and come to an agreement on price before they list it so that they can save some commission. Overall, though, I would not spend too much time going after FSBOs unless you have some type of insider information.

## 52. How Much Should I Budget Once I Move In?

Buying a house is a large investment – for most people, the most significant investment of their lives. You need to make sure not to stretch yourself too thin. Most experts recommend having a rainy-day fund of at least six months' worth of income. This could be for maintenance repairs, upgrades, as well as the unlikely event of a job loss or another issue. It is smart to have the money in an easily accessible, i.e., liquid, fund.

That doesn't mean you shouldn't buy a house if you don't have six months of reserves, but make sure you are not spending every last penny on the property because there are always unexpected things that can arise. One thing I can guarantee is that you will want to do upgrades and repairs. They may not be the biggest ticket items, but as you live in a house, you start to get ideas for projects – whether it's cosmetic or something that needs to be repaired. You will be spending extra money on your house one way or another.

## 53. Which Direction Is The Market Headed?

There is no way to 100% predict where the real estate market is headed. Don't let any agent tell you otherwise! However, that being said, we can look at historical trends to get a general idea of what might happen in the next five to 10 years.

According to Forbes, since the Great Depression, there are recessions every seven to 12 years. By doing some quick online research, you can find out when the last recession was and where the market could be headed in the following years. One thing I can 100% predict is that the real estate market is cyclical, so you can always try to time it.

What I do know, though, is that if you focus on buying in the right location, it does not matter what part of the cycle you buy in because the value will always be there. When the recession hit in 2007, people who bought McMansions 45 minutes outside of the city were hit hard and lost hundreds of thousands of equity.

However, people that bought smaller properties in the downtown and up-and-coming areas in the city rebounded quickly and did not even see that much of a housing crash. The best way to protect your investment is to spend a bit more and buy in the right location rather than buying a beautiful house in the middle of nowhere.

## 54. Should I Buy A House With A Friend?

If you live in an expensive market, then purchasing a property might seem like a pipe dream of sorts. However, if you have a friend who is in the same situation, it can be tempting to look into buying a place together. By pooling your resources and income, you could potentially qualify for a nice property in your ideal area. Instead of paying rent, you both could start to build up equity.

Now, while I have seen this work out before, I would strongly suggest that you really think about the decision. Buying a house is very different from moving into a rental with your friend. You should plan on living there for a minimum of three years, and better yet, five or more to see the buildup in equity.

Additionally, if the property does not appreciate and one person wants to sell, then you may be forced to come out of pocket with cash. Life situations change all the time, and maybe one party might move out across the country and rent their part of the house out. There could be a million scenarios that could play out. There are also repairs and maintenance that you don't think about when you are a renter.

Overall, this strategy of buying together has worked for some people, but I would recommend you get a lawyer to draw up an agreement and really think about if you want to be locked in with this person for the next three to seven years.

## 55. What Are Zestimates? Are They Accurate?

Zestimates are Zillow's estimate for a property based on a proprietary formula. According to Zillow, the majority of the time (75%), their estimate is within 10% of the final sales price. I like to use the Zestimate for a ballpark price range of a property, but I would not rely on it to make offers. It is never as accurate as recent comparable sales that your agent will pull for you.

Since the Zestimate takes into account all the properties in the vicinity, you want to be sure you are running comps only on the specific type of property (for example, townhouse) and ideally, in the same subdivision. As an investor, I like using Zestimates, though, because I know that if a seller wants to get rid of a property for let's say 200K and the Zestimate is 300K, then chances are it could be a good deal. I still run my own exact numbers, but it lets me know that the deal has potential.

## 56. Is The Market Overpriced?

For as long as I have been in real estate, I have always heard that the market is overpriced. Even during the 2009 recession, when prices were at rock bottom, I remember investors and other buyers were still worried the market was overpriced. When you start comparing prices from the year before, five years before, or even 10 years before, it can drive you crazy, thinking that you are now overpaying for properties.

I remember an older associate of mine sharing a story with me that I'll never forget. He had the opportunity to purchase the neighbor's house in the 1980s for 70K or something low like that, and my associate was financially able to do it except for one thing. He believed that 70K was way overpriced for the neighborhood. Well, that same area now has houses for two million dollars. Just the piece of land itself is worth near a million dollars to a builder.

The lesson I got is that, no matter what part of the economic cycle you are in, and especially if you are a first-time home buyer, the market always seems overpriced. The way to counterbalance that is buying in a prime area or transitional area that has a lot of development going on in and around it. If you buy too far outside of the city, you are less insulated from market downturns. Location is everything when it comes to real estate. If you want your property value to hold up or increase, make sure to buy in or around the city areas.

## 57. What Is The Commute Time?

I touched on this briefly earlier but when it comes to buying a house, you must do research on how long your commute will be. That means not only online research with Google maps and the traffic patterns of that area, but also driving the commute or reading forums about the commute.

I remember helping a client buy a house for someone that was selling after only one year. I asked the agent why they were selling so quickly. Apparently, the buyers had purchased the home from overseas and were unaware of how long their commute would be. Their two-hour daily commute got old pretty quickly, and they ended up selling at a discount so they could be closer to work. Don't make that same mistake!

## 58. Can I Get Rid Of Cigarette Smoke Or Other Smells?

I have seen this scenario happen many times. You find a great-looking property, but for some reason, it has been listed on the market for a while and is a good amount below the comps in price. You immediately ask your real estate agent to show you the property, only to find out when you walk in that the property reeks of cigarettes.

What do you do in this situation? In terms of resale value and general livability, the property will obviously need some work to remove the smell before you move in. We usually tell clients that it is possible to get rid of the smell, but it is not guaranteed that you can remove it.

As a real estate investor, I would have no problem moving into a house with cigarette smell. I hate cigarettes, but there are so many products nowadays for removing those kinds of smells that

I would not mind, as long as I got the house at the right price.

If you search online, you will find tens of thousands of articles on removing the smell. Some of the basic things you should do include removing all the carpet, drapes, and furniture. Then you should open all the windows, turn on all the fans, and start washing all the interior walls and surfaces. Then you would repaint the house, change light fixtures, wash windows, get the vents professionally cleaned, and possibly even get an air purifier. There are countless other things you can do as well.

While this may sound like a lot to do, it's really just cleaning, repainting, and some additional things. As I said, I would have no problem moving into a house that smells of cigarettes since it most likely could be bought at a discount. However, if you are hypersensitive to cigarettes, then you should do more research.

## 59. Should I Buy In A Transitional Neighborhood?

As a real estate investor and broker, I think buying in a transitional neighborhood is one of the best investments you can make. A transitional neighborhood is usually an older neighborhood that was once known as a bad area but is now going through a revival.

Here are some traits of transitional neighborhoods.

1) The first trait is obvious. If you drive through the community, you will see a lot of construction going on. This could be large renovations of older houses as well as new developments next to the older homes and buildings.

2) The next trait is that these neighborhoods are accessible. They are close to the downtown core of the neighborhood and have public transportation options, such as a local train or subway.

3) The third trait is that these neighborhoods are right next to the hot neighborhoods. It is common for the hot neighborhoods'

development to spill over into the transitional areas.

4) The crime rate is going down. If you look up articles of the neighborhood, you should be able to find lots of info on crime, and hopefully articles and stats on how the crime has gone down over the last five, 10, or 15 years.

5) The fifth trait is that the neighborhood might have an arts or cultural scene. For some reason, artists are great at finding the next cool and currently inexpensive neighborhood.

6) Another prime trait is that the neighborhood has a lot of historic architecture and character. According to the book Zillow Talk, "The older the average is, the more likely a given neighborhood will see strong appreciation."

7) Lastly, if you see a Starbucks, or even better, a Whole Foods move into the neighborhood, that is a good sign. These companies spend tens of millions of dollars trying to find the next hot neighborhoods and have a specific

algorithm for doing so. Rely on their research for your next home purchase. If you want to see your property appreciate, then buy in a transitional neighborhood. If you want a beautiful house that is ready for move-in far out in the suburbs, then that's fine, but don't expect it to appreciate as much.

## 60. How Do I Know If A Crime Was Committed In The House?

Most states do not require that a real estate agent provide that information. However, you can find out a ton about a property by just Googling the address. Most of the time, the address will show the Zillow, Redfin, and other real estate data. However, every now and then, there will be articles that mention the property.

This can give you more insight before making your offer. Just make sure you Google the house before buying it and not after purchasing it. You can also Google the numerical block of the street, for example, 500 block of Main Street, instead of Googling the specific address because you will get more search results for that on Google. With crimes, fires, and other notable incidences, the police reports and newspapers usually just give the block of the street and not the specific address, for privacy reasons.

## 61. Is The Neighborhood Safe?

Most real estate agents are not able to answer this question because it could be violating fair housing laws. The best way to find out about a neighborhood is by looking at the crime report online, reading articles about the area, driving through it at night, jogging or biking through the neighborhood, and talking to neighbors.

Some neighbors love to talk and will tell you the history of the neighborhood, while others won't want to talk to you at all. Find the neighbor that knows everything and get a rundown of the area. Keep in mind, every neighborhood has some type of crime throughout a year, so I would focus on the overall trends in the crime rate if you are looking at buying in an up-and-coming area.

SECTION 6

---

# Making Offers and Negotiating

## 62. What Is An Earnest Money Deposit (EMD)?

An earnest money deposit or EMD is what you put down with the title company or real estate brokerage once you go under contract. It goes towards your down payment and closing costs and is usually about 2% of the purchase price. In a competitive situation with multiple offers, you should consider putting a larger earnest money deposit down, closer to 5%.

Most real estate contracts give you five days from the day you go under contract to deposit the earnest money. Always check via phone instead of email with your title company or broker before depositing the money. There are a lot of phishing scams out there these days.

If your deal falls out of contract and you withdraw your offer within your allotted contingency times, then you can get your full earnest money deposit back. However, keep in mind that both buyer and seller have to sign to release the funds if you do back out of the contract. If you try to withdraw your offer after your contingency periods have expired, then you are putting your earnest money deposit at serious risk and can lose the full amount.

## 63. When Making An Offer, What Contingencies Should I Have?

The type of contingencies that you have with an offer depends on how competitive the property is. In a standard offer, you will have the home inspection contingency, financing contingency, and appraisal contingency. If the property is in a condo or HOA, then you will usually have a three- to five-day contingency period to review the condo and HOA docs as well.

The home inspection contingency is the most significant contingency because that's when you find out what kind of house you could be buying. The contingency will allow you to negotiate for repairs or credits, or simply cancel the contract based on the findings of the inspector.

The financing and appraisal contingencies are less in your control since it is the lender that is approving your financing and an appraisal company running their own numbers. In the unlikely event that your financing is rejected, you can withdraw your offer without losing your earnest money deposit.

If you are in a competitive situation with multiple offers, we usually recommend dropping your financing and appraisal contingencies and doing a pre-inspection so that you can remove that contingency when making your offer. A pre-inspection is an inspection done before you make an offer. Always talk to your lender before dropping the financing contingency. By lowering or removing your contingencies, you can make your offer significantly more attractive in the eyes of the seller.

## 64. How Do I Win In A Multiple-Offer Scenario?

In a multiple-offer scenario, there are a few things you should do. To begin with, make sure your agent is in constant communication to get an idea of exactly how many offers there are, how competitive the offers are (i.e., are people dropping contingencies, doing pre-inspections, are there cash offers, etc.), and what type of offer the seller would prefer. Sometimes a seller might need a rent back or might need to close in three weeks, and many other scenarios. You can craft the best offer by knowing the seller's needs.

The first thing you should have is a preapproval letter from a local lender. If you just have a national preapproval letter with a 1-800 number to call, your offer will look significantly weaker than if you got pre-approved by a local lender with a cell phone and email address.

Next, you could increase your earnest money deposit. Most earnest money deposits are around 2-3%. You could increase yours to 5% or even more. After that, I would recommend getting a pre-inspection.

This is where you pay a home inspector before you even make the offer to do an inspection so that you can find out if you should waive the contingency. By removing the home inspection contingency, you will make your offer much more enticing since inspections are usually the biggest hang-up between buyers and sellers.

Next, you should consider waiving your appraisal contingency. This means that, if the property does not appraise, you will have to come out of pocket to make up the difference. You can also do a partial appraisal contingency, where you put in that the appraisal contingency will be released as long as the property appraises for at least 500K or whatever price you feel comfortable with.

Finally, you should talk to your lender to see if they feel comfortable dropping your financing contingency. If they tell you that you are a slam dunk to get approved, then I would strongly consider that. However, if you are pulling together every last dollar you have to make the deal work, then I would not recommend dropping this contingency.

In addition to dropping or lowering your contingencies, you should consider doing an escalation clause of 1K-3K above any other offer with a cap that you feel comfortable at. If the seller goes with your escalated offer, they have to send you a copy of the offer that triggered your escalation.

In conclusion, your agent should be in constant communication with the listing agent, you should have a strong local preapproval letter, you should increase your earnest money deposit, get a pre-inspection done, waive your financing contingency after speaking with your lender, waive your appraisal contingency, do an escalation clause, and lastly, you can write a personal letter to the seller about how much you want the house. There are plenty of "letter to seller" templates online that you can customize. By doing all of the aforementioned things, you can drastically improve your chances of being the winning bidder.

## 65. What Is A Seller Disclosure?

When you buy a house that is listed, a seller disclosure is a standard form where the seller has to disclose any known defects – current or past – about the property. Each state has different requirements as far as disclosures go. Some states are buyer beware states, where the seller is basically selling the house in as-is condition and does not have to mention anything, while other states have an itemized list of parts of the house and whether they've had any issues.

You should receive the disclosure form before making your offer, so you can review. However, in some cases such as foreclosures, inherited homes, or properties, where they have not owned the house for very long, the seller might not have to disclose anything. While most sellers disclose all the information, every now and then, sellers might try to leave some information out.

It is always best to get a thorough home inspection done in addition to reviewing any disclosures. A home inspector will be able to find any (potential) issues since they are going through the entire home and testing everything.

They will be able to find if there have been repairs done or covered up, and more. If you believe the seller covered something up, it can be difficult to prove they knew about it before, so that's why you should get an inspection done and find out about anything before closing.

Some savvy buyers might talk to the neighbors to find out additional information if they suspect anything. However, keep in mind, when buying a house, there are always unexpected repairs, and it does mean the seller was hiding something. If you get a good inspector and budget in a reserve fund for updates and house maintenance, you should not have any issues.

## 66. What If The Seller Needs Time After Closing To Move?

Sometimes, when you buy a house, the seller may request a "rent back," where the seller stays in the property for an additional few days or, in some cases, up to a month or so. Rent backs are common. You just have to work out your schedule and come to an agreement with the sellers beforehand to make sure there is no confusion. If you do agree to a rent back, your real estate agent will have an addendum that specifies the final date the sellers have to move out and the amount per day that the rent back will cost them.

Usually, the seller will pay your PITI, which is the cost of your mortgage plus interest plus taxes so that it won't cost you anything. The title company will determine exactly how much that is.

In a competitive situation with multiple offers, it is not uncommon to offer the seller a free rent back for a few days or even a month. You will also do two walk-throughs, one on the day of closing, when the seller will most likely still have all their stuff in the house, and then another one once they move out.

## 67. What Happens If I Get Buyer's Remorse?

Occasionally, first-time home buyers might get buyer's remorse. This is common, so don't freak out. You have made a large purchase, so there is always a part of you that has some hesitation. The first way to not get buyer's remorse is to know exactly what you are looking for. This sounds obvious, but I've seen many buyers who bought one of the first couple of houses they saw instead of doing a more thorough search.

I always recommend checking out many different styles, price ranges, and even areas so that you can really hone down on what type of property you are looking for. Many people end up changing their mind on the style of house once they see it in person. So make sure you check out a ton of open houses and do a good amount of online research about neighborhoods, styles of homes, and the overall home-buying experience.

Sometimes buyers think they are overpaying for properties. I would just say, generally speaking, everybody thinks they are overpaying for properties and people have been saying this for the longest time. If you are looking back to five or 10 years ago to see what these types of properties used to sell for, then you can't compare them to today's prices.

The real estate market moves in cycles but goes up over time. An appraiser still has to verify that the price you are paying for the house is worth it and historically prices go up. So long as you buy in a good area that holds value, it doesn't even matter if you overpaid. You'll set a new price for comps and more places will sell for that price or above.

Lastly, once you buy a house, stop looking at other properties. There will always be properties coming and going, and it is very easy to think that you might have wanted another one that just went on the market. The grass is always greener on the other side, so stop browsing listings after you buy. It will drive you crazy.

All this being said, you should have a level of excitement when buying a property and you should congratulate yourself, not get remorse when it comes to buying a house. If there is some serious issue with the house, then you should cancel it within the home inspection contingency period, which is usually seven to 10 days after going under contract.

## 68. How Do I Cancel A Contract?

Nearly every standard contract comes with several contingencies, including the home inspection, appraisal, and financing. The home inspection is your best option for canceling a contract. Most inspection contingencies are about seven to 10 days and give you an out clause. Even if the house is in perfect condition, you are still allowed to cancel for any reason based on the home inspection within that time frame.

If you are buying a condo, townhouse, or single-family house with an HOA, then you typically have three days from receiving the condo or HOA documents to cancel for any reason. Outside of these two contingencies, it is complicated to cancel a contract without putting your earnest money deposit at risk.

## 69. Should I Send A Lowball Offer?

Lowball offers have a time and place in real estate. If a property has been sitting on the market for a long time and needs work or the listing says "motivated seller," "bring all offers," "estate sale," "TLC needed," or anything like that, those are good signs that the seller could entertain a lowball offer. If a property has only been on the market for a short while (a month or a couple of months) and there are no obvious signs that the seller is looking to get rid of it, then you could still send in a lowball offer, but it might not be taken seriously.

A lowball offer is anything under 10% of the current asking price. However, sometimes sellers know a property is overpriced and are just testing the market. If all the comps support a much lower price, first have your agent get an idea from the listing agent how flexible the seller might be and then submit your offer.

Also, when you are in the price range of over 1M, it is not uncommon for properties to drop over 100K from 1.3 to 1.2, or even 1.1M. In that price range, there are significantly fewer buyers and the price is more subjective.

## 70. Can I Make Changes To The Contract After Going Under Contract?

Yes and no. Once you go under contract, any change you make has to be approved by the seller. Some items that are commonly changed include adding a buyer's name to a contract since that would not affect the sale in any way and changing the title company. These are all relatively minor changes that a seller usually approves.

In terms of changing major things like closing dates or other changes like that you still need to get the seller's approval and it's not always a guaranteed. Any time you are making changes to a contract after going under contract, it is a bit of a red flag. You lose a little bit of leverage with the seller every time you decide you want to change something. The best practice is to have your terms, price, and contingencies all ready from the start so that you don't have to make any changes.

## 71. Can I Write My Own Language Into The Contract?

Many times, first-time home buyers will want to rewrite specific language in the contract, especially lawyers. What you need to know is that the standard real estate contracts have been used tens of thousands of times and no seller will take your offer seriously if you decide you want to rewrite the standard contract.

As a buyer, you can always write in whatever clauses you want, such as "this offer expires at 10 a.m. on Tuesday" or "seller to remove playground in the backyard." However, as far as rewriting contracts goes, I would stay away from it. There's no reason to do it, and it will just make things more complicated.

## 72. What Is Negotiable In Real Estate?

Technically speaking, everything is negotiable in real estate. The overwhelming majority of the time, the most significant negotiation points are price, closing date, and home inspection items. That being said, you could request that the seller have their home theatre system convey, hot tub convey, or any number of things.

I would focus your negotiation on the biggest parts of the transaction, such as the price, as opposed to getting bogged down in smaller things like removing a flower pot from the back patio, but I have certainly seen it all.

## 73. Is Price Per Square Foot Accurate?

When looking at comps and coming up with a price to offer, one way is looking at comparable price per square foot in that area. Usually, the only time we use price per square foot to evaluate a property is if the property is a condo or townhouse, and you are comparing units in the same building.

For example, if you are in downtown Manhattan, price per square foot is what everybody uses for comps. However, if you are looking at single-family houses in the suburbs, there are just too many variables, such as the lot, finishes, style of home, how busy the street is, the school district, and more, that go into determining a price than using price per square foot model.

Additionally, if you are looking at buildings in a downtown area, they will have different amenities, condo fees, parking, views, and other variables that make it difficult to rely on price per square foot. I like to use price per square foot when dealing with condos, but only after looking at recently sold properties of the same style and only if it's in the same or similar buildings.

## 74. What Questions Should I Ask Before Making An Offer?

Before making an offer, you should find out these critical pieces of information. And if the seller does not know the answers, plan on spending some money to replace them in the next five or 10 years. You should first figure out if they've done any renovations, as well as the age of the major systems such as the HVAC and roof. Most of the time, an HVAC can last 15-20 years and a roof 25-35 years. Those are typically the two most significant expenses for first-time home buyers.

Next, you should find out if they currently have any offers or have had any previous offers that they rejected. Once you get the listing agent to start talking, they will often provide additional information that you didn't even ask for but that can help you craft a better offer.

Lastly, you should ask for the seller's ideal closing scenario since some sellers might need a shorter or longer closing date.

## 75. How Long Does The Seller Have To Respond To Your Offer?

In most of our contracts, we state that we "request the seller to respond within 24 hours."

That does not mean the contract automatically expires after 24 hours; it is more of a friendly request.

Sometimes the seller is out of town, older, a separated couple, or they do not check their email very often, and it can take several days to get a response since they have to think about it. Other times, the agent might be trying to round up other potential buyers that saw the property to let them know there is an offer and if they are interested, to submit ASAP. I like to put pressure on the agent to get a response sooner rather than later.

## 76. How Does Real Estate Negotiation Work?

When you make an offer, the seller will accept your offer, counter your offer, or not even respond at all if the offer is too low. Typically, there will be some negotiation back and forth. If the property has been listed on the market for a long time or needs a lot of work, there might be some more room for negotiation. Your buyer's agent should be able to get a sense of the amount of negotiation room available before submitting an offer and of course you can still submit whatever price you want.

I like to personally find out the seller's ideal closing scenario before submitting any offer. Properties that have just been listed on the market or are under 30 days on the market generally don't have as much room for negotiation. The seller should usually respond to your offer within a day or two unless they are out of town or have another reason. If you can't come to an agreement on price you should still keep an eye on the property because every now and then it will sit on the market and the seller will have to drop the price down.

## 77. How Much Should I Offer?

This depends on a lot of factors, but I will break it down. From doing your own research, you should have a general idea of what those type of properties sell for in that area. Additionally, before you make an offer, your real estate agent will send you comparable sales and give you their opinion of what they think it's worth and what you should offer.

If it looks like there will be multiple offers, you will most likely have to consider dropping contingencies such as appraisal and financing, and just doing a limited pass/fail home inspection as well as an escalation clause.

If the property has been listed for more than a couple of weeks, your agent should reach out to the listing agent and find out if they have had any offers, what the seller's ideal closing scenario is, and how motivated they are. In many cases, sellers do not drop their price too much during the first month, even if the property is clearly overpriced.

I would not offer the full price for anything that has been listed for more than a month unless its an unusual situation. That's not to say I would throw out a lowball offer either. You would have to look at the comparable sales and come in below asking price, while considering what properties have sold for recently. I would also keep in all your standard contingencies if the property has been on the market for at least a month.

# SECTION 7

# Inspections

## 78. Should I Get A Home Inspection?

If you are a first-time home buyer, I would absolutely recommend getting a home inspection. The inspection will teach you a lot, and the inspector will alert you to any serious problems as well as general maintenance tips. Additionally, when you do a home inspection, you will come up with a list of repairs or credits that the seller could be willing to do.

There are only a couple of times when I would recommend waiving a home inspection. The first is if you are in a competitive situation with multiple offers, you should consider doing a pre-inspection.

This is where you pay the inspector before making an offer so that you can waive that contingency if the report comes back with only minor issues. Many buyers try to waive as many contingencies as possible when there are multiple offers.

Another situation where you can waive an inspection is if you get a terrific deal. I've bought several properties where the numbers were so good that I didn't care if the entire house needed to be renovated. That's how low the price was. In that scenario, I don't burden a seller with a home inspection.

However, for any property that is listed on the MLS, a home inspection is standard. Your real estate agent should have a list of recommended home inspectors for you, and countless websites have reviews of local home inspectors. Plan on spending about $500 per inspection for a normal-sized home or up to $1,000 if it's a large 5,000-square foot house.

## 79. What Happens If The Inspection Reveals Issues?

No matter if you get a home inspection for a brand-new single-family house, studio condo, or another type of property, you will have a 30- or even 40-page home inspection report. I have been on countless inspections, and I can guarantee you the home inspector will find items, even on brand-new homes. It is your home inspector and your agent's job to tell you what is common versus what is a serious issue.

If you have never bought a house before, it can be very intimidating to get your first inspection report back because you'll think the entire home needs to be rebuilt. Don't freak out; the inspector is playing devil's advocate and usually errs on the conservative side of things because they don't want to be held liable for missing anything. A good home inspector will take detailed notes with pictures and have a summary of items at the end of the report that tells you what is serious, what is just older, and what are minor cosmetic issues.

Most sellers only fix something or give a credit for something if it is broken or a "major issue." If your AC works great, but it is older, a seller does not typically replace it for you. Usually, you will go back to the seller requesting that they have a licensed contractor who specializes in the issue (i.e., electrician, plumber, etc.) evaluate and repair any items that were flagged.

Every house has something. Typically, the seller will either give a credit or offer to hire a contractor to fix any issues as long as they are reasonable. I recommend getting a credit because it makes the transaction cleaner. Sometimes repairs are very relative, so it can cause a headache when you are getting to closing, and one party is saying they did the repair and the other party is saying they didn't fully complete the repair to their standards.

## 80. How Do I Make Sure Renovations Were Done Correctly?

If you are buying a house that has had a lot of renovations done on it, there are several things you should do to ensure the work was done correctly. For starters, you should get a highly recommended and thorough home inspector to give you a report on the property. Home inspectors usually err on the side of caution, so if they see anything a little bit out of order, they will flag it on their report.

Next, you should make sure that all proper permits were pulled and that they were closed out. A quick search on your county's website should let you pull up the permit history of the work done and if it was closed out or not. You don't want any open permits when buying a house.

Lastly, if the work was done recently, the seller should be able to provide some paperwork on the renovations done, and at the very least, what company or contractors worked on the property. This could give you some reassurance if the work was done by a local contractor with a good reputation.

All that being said, I would rely mostly on the home inspector. It's not uncommon for people to not get permits for different renovations, especially if the work was done a while ago, but that does not mean the house is about to fall apart. Verify with your home inspector if any of the work done needs anything additional to make it function correctly or if there are any hazards with the current setup of the house.

## 81. Should I Get An Inspection On A New Construction Home?

Yes, I would highly recommend getting a home inspection done on a new construction home. You want to be sure the builder did not take any shortcuts. Additionally, many times with new construction, the builder is much more likely to fix all the items you find because they still have their construction crew there and might be working on other houses in the neighborhood.

While I generally see much fewer issues with new construction homes, I have been on several home inspections with new construction properties that found numerous items that needed to be fixed.

## 82. Should I Get A Radon Test?

When you get a home inspection, I would almost always recommend getting a radon test done as well. Radon is the second leading cause of lung cancer in the United States. Some states, such as Pennsylvania, can have extremely high and unsafe levels. You can buy kits at Home Depot and online for $20 to test the levels yourself.

However, given the seriousness of radon, I would just pay the $150 for a professional company to test and evaluate it for you. There is a lot of information online about radon, including a radon map by the EPA that shows what areas have higher concentrations of radon.

If you are in a first floor condo or a property that doesn't have a basement, the chances are much less likely that you have radon, but I would still get a test done.

Fortunately, radon is relatively easy to remediate. It usually costs about $1,000 and is a PVC pipe with a fan that is attached to the side of the house. If radon is discovered, the seller almost always will pay a radon remediation company to install a system or give you a credit for it. Standard real estate contracts also have a radon clause in addition to the home inspection clause, so you will be covered in the event of radon.

## 83. How Can I Find A Great Contractor?

There are three strategies I like to use for finding a contractor when I am working on a property. They are all simple and effective.

The first strategy can be done in your day-to-day activities. After you have purchased a property, when you are walking around your neighborhood or driving around, you will see different properties that are being worked on.

Contractors typically have their sign out in the front yard or at least their vehicle with their contact information. This is the first way to start building a list. You want to look for contractors that are busy because that means they do a good job, and local, because that means they will know the specifics to the style and age of your property.

Next, you should ask for as many referrals as possible from friends, real estate agents, or even local community events. You never want to be the first person to use a contractor, so if they come highly recommended and they have good reviews online, chances are they will do an excellent job for you.

Lastly, I like to use online sites like Angie's List or other review sites where contractors run different specials for kitchen renovations, bathrooms, floors, and nearly any repair. The great thing about Angie's List is that the vendors are licensed and insured, and you will see tons of reviews on the work they have done. This will help you in your decision.

By using those three strategies, you should be able to build a master list of contractors. I always recommend getting three bids for any project. You would be shocked at how different the estimates will be. Lastly, before hiring any contractor, make sure they are licensed and insured, and they should be able to provide that information with no issue.

## 84. Is The Crack A Foundational Crack Or Just Cosmetic?

Generally speaking, most first-time home buyers are worried about foundational issues when buying a home. From having looked at thousands of houses and bought countless others, I can tell you that foundational problems are extremely rare. While they are certainly out there, the overwhelming majority of the cracks you might see in a house are standard and what's called settling.

The one time I was buying a house with a structural issue, it was obvious. There was a massive tree pushing on the foundational wall of the front of the house, and in the basement, the entire wall looked like it was ready to burst. Hairline cracks are not foundational issues.

That being said, you should always get a home inspection if you are a first-time home buyer and ask your inspector about the cracks if you have them. Home inspectors err on the side of caution, so if they see anything that looks remotely concerning, they will recommend getting a specialist to look at it, and you can usually extend your contingency.

Additionally, even if you end up buying a house with a structural issue, they are typically fixable. For a serious foundational problem, I would estimate at least $15,000. However, some investors I know prefer to buy properties with structural issues because it eliminates 99% of the other buyers out there.

Since they know how much structural repairs cost, they can run their numbers to make it work. Most people think the entire house needs to be torn down with structural issues, when in reality, it's usually not that bad.

## 85. Should I Ask For Repairs Or A Credit?

When you buy a house, you almost always do a home inspection. Just about every house, even new construction, has a list of items to fix. Some of them might be serious; others might be minor or even cosmetic. That being said, the seller – and many times, the buyer – prefer to do a credit in lieu of the items because of the hassle involved with hiring different contractors to get work done before closing and meeting the standards of the buyer.

I have seen it happen numerous times that the buyer opts to have items fixed instead of a credit. The seller hires a licensed contractor to perform the repairs, but right before closing, the repairs do not meet the satisfaction of the buyer, and it turns into a big headache.

That is why I usually recommend doing a credit in lieu of any items and have the seller address anything with a licensed contractor only if it's a significant issue. For example, in an older house, the inspector may have flagged 15 or 20 items.

Instead of asking for different contractors to fix all 20 items, you would check with your real estate agent and come up with a credit for the majority or all of the issues. The end home inspection would say, "in lieu of items XXXXX, seller to credit buyer $7,000," or whatever number makes sense.

Similar to when you made the offer to purchase, you should probably start your repairs request a little bit aggressively, knowing that you can come down a bit. Don't start too aggressively, such as asking a 50K credit/price reduction for a brand-new house because many times the seller will come back just as aggressively and the deal will fall apart. You need to find a middle ground of reasonable repairs and/or credits based on current defects in the property and not just upgrades that you want to see happen.

# SECTION 8

---

# The Final Steps of Closing the Deal

## 86. How Do I Avoid Junk Fees?

When buying a property for the first time, the number of fees included in a purchase can be a little overwhelming. However, that does not necessarily mean they are all junk fees. The best way to ensure that you don't get any junk fees added to your price is to get at least three estimates from recommended local mortgage brokers. They will all have slightly different prices and rates. If you see anything unusual, then be sure to mention it. In some cases, the fees can be negotiable.

Take solace in the fact that, since the subprime meltdown of 2007, the real estate industry has changed significantly. It is now much more strict about junk fees. If you have any questions, be sure to bring them up with your agent, lender, and title company.

Your best bet is to shop around at a couple of lenders, title companies, and ask your real estate agent what fees they have. On the real estate agent side of things, some brokerages are notorious for charging admin or brokerage fees in the range of $300-$500, which can usually be removed if you ask your agent. They should not be charging you these without at least disclosing them at first. And, since your buyer's agent should be making a nice commission on the sale, they should have no problem paying that fee themselves.

## 87. What Is A Loan Estimate?

The loan estimate has replaced the truth in lending disclosure and is a three-page form that you receive after applying for a mortgage. It gives you all the critical information related to your loan costs, including interest rate, monthly payment, closing costs, taxes, insurance, and other relevant information.

The loan estimate was created to help you better understand and make your loan clearer. It is a standard form that is required by all lenders. This also makes it easier for you as a consumer when you are comparing mortgage loans.

A loan estimate is free; however, you might be required to pay for a credit check when applying. These are also not the final terms of the loan, but if anything changes with your loan, the lender is required to send you the final closing disclosure at least three days before closing. The loan estimate cannot be higher than the original quote to you, except in certain costs related to changing the type of loan, reducing your down payment, significant changes to your credit score, or not locking in your rate.

## 88. What Is A Closing Disclosure Form?

A closing disclosure or CD is a five-page document from your lender that gives you final details about your mortgage and the costs associated with it. Your lender is required by law to give it to you at least three days before closing so that you can compare it to their original loan estimate.

This three-day buffer also allows you to tie up any loose ends and ask your lender and title company any additional questions. The CD used to be known as the HUD-1, which was a longer and more confusing document that only had to be provided on the day of closing. The CD is more streamlined. Make sure you go over it in the three-day window to check whether everything is what you thought it would be.

## 89. What Is A Home Warranty And Should I Get One?

A home warranty is a product you purchase before or after closing that covers major appliances and systems in your house in case they break down. There are different types of coverage policies, but they usually cover significant appliances, your HVAC system, hot water heater, electrical, plumbing, and in some cases, the roof and more. They typically cost around $500. Sometimes a seller will include a home warranty with the sale of the house. Home warranties can give a first-time home buyer peace of mind when they move into a property because there are no major cost surprises.

There is some debate, however, as to whether they are worth it or not. If you are buying a newer property, it often already comes with warranties from the manufacturer and/or builder. However, with older homes, it could be a good idea. If something in your property does break, you file a claim and pay a fee for a contractor to evaluate and repair the system or issue.

The downsides with home warranties are that you don't get to choose what contractor or company comes out. Also, warranty companies are known for fixing issues and not necessarily replacing items.

So you should not expect a brand-new HVAC or refrigerator if you start having problems with either. Additionally, you could make the argument that a homeowner would be better off spending the $500 cost of a warranty and service fee if something were to break into upgrading or replacing the issue as opposed to putting a quick fix on it.

As an experienced real estate broker and investor, I usually prefer to receive a credit in the amount of a home warranty instead of an actual warranty. However, if you are a first-time home buyer and you are buying an older house, it can certainly give you more peace of mind.

## 90. Should I Have A Real Estate Attorney Look Over Documents?

Many first-time home buyers think they need to have an attorney look over every document. Honestly, I think that is a bit of overkill. If you are using a standard real estate agent contract for your jurisdiction, there is not much you can or should change. These are standard contracts that have been used tens of thousands of times.

If you ever have questions, you can always ask your title company since they are required to have an attorney on staff for legal questions, issues, and closings. The only time I would have a real estate attorney take a second look at any documents is if you were using a non-standard real estate contract, if there was a legal issue, or if you were buying some type of commercial real estate or big project instead of just a house, condo, or townhome.

Better yet, do your own research, ask the local attorney at your title company, and ask your experienced real estate agent. By doing all three, you should be able to come up with a solution.

## 91. How Does The Final Walk-Through Work?

You typically schedule a walk-through on the day of closing, several hours before you sign your closing documents. Walk-throughs are straightforward. You walk through the house and test all the appliances, test the HVAC, run all the water in the house, and make sure the house is in the same condition as it was before. If there is a repair list, then you match up the receipts and verify whether the work was done.

If there are a lot of repairs that were agreed on, then I would recommend doing a final walk-through a couple of days before closing. That way, if there are any disagreements on the repairs, you have enough time to get them worked out. That's also why I would recommend getting a credit in lieu of having lots of repairs, because in many cases it turns into a situation where there are disagreements as to whether the repair was done correctly. The last thing you want is a headache right before closing, so when in doubt, opt for the repair credit.

Every now and then, something is damaged or maybe the seller still has some things to move. That is why you should carefully look at the home inspection report before doing the walk-through, so you know if there are any differences.

Normal wear and tear such as small scratches or paint missing from where a TV was removed are not considered significant to warrant an addendum. However, if the AC is not turning on, the projector TV system that was agreed to convey is missing, or there's a broken window or things like that, then you would do a walk-through addendum that mentions the repairs.

You would have the seller sign it, and the addendum would carry through closing. That means they would get it fixed as soon as possible, ideally within the next seven to 14 days since sometimes contractors are booked for a while.

Overall, though, walk-throughs are usually smooth and straightforward. If you are not sure about their repairs, then book the walk-through a few days closing.

## 92. How Does Closing Work?

Closing works in a straightforward way. Your title company of choice and your real estate agent should have a couple recommendations will schedules with you the time and the place for closing. Many title companies require that you sign the paperwork in their office, although just as many will meet you at the property after walk-through to sign the closing documents.

You will need to bring your ID as well as a cashier's check or certified check with you. Your title company will also verify several days or, better yet, a week in advance that they have everything they need from you. All you have to do now is sign. If you have any questions, it's better to call them rather than email them because of all the phishing scams out there.

At closing, it is usually just the closing or title agent, you the buyer, and your real estate agent.

Nowadays, closings are usually done separately to save time and to avoid any awkwardness if it's been a contentious negotiation. If you are a buyer, the closing will take about 45 minutes, so it's not like it should take all day or anything, as most people think. You will get the keys at the closing table, and the property will be yours.

If you are out of town for the scheduled closing date, you can appoint a power of attorney form for someone else to sign in your place. You can also sign your side of the documents in advance and send them back to the title company. A good title company will be as accommodating as possible to make it work, and many title companies have multiple branch offices to assist you if needed.

## 93. What Will The Closing Costs Be? Who Pays For Them?

When you make an offer, you should expect to pay about 3% of the purchase price in closing costs. Every area is different, though. In some extreme cases, closing costs can be closer to 5% of the purchase price, so always check with your lender. Closing costs include things like mortgage application fees, appraisal fee, title fees, title insurance, transfer and recordation taxes, and other items. Title companies offer different prices on their services, though I would recommend going with a highly rated company versus a discount company when it comes to title work.

With closings, it's nice to have everything go smoothly and not have last-minute delays or issues arise that can derail a closing. In some cases, a seller will pay for a certain amount of your closing costs. This needs to be specified when you make your offer, and it's not uncommon for the seller to give some type of subsidy.

Just make sure your lender is aware of the subsidy because you can't have the seller subsidy be more than the seller closing costs. Keep in mind that, to the seller, it's all about net sales price, so an offer of let's say 300K with a 10K subsidy is essentially the same as a 290K offer with no subsidy.

## 94. What Is A Title Search?

Once you get a property under contract, the first

thing your agent will do is send the copy of the ratified contract to the title company so they can get started with the title search. A title search usually takes a least a week or two. The title company will search back to see if there are any taxes owed or liens, and check public records, the recorder of deeds, and any other necessary information.

It is not uncommon for the title company to find smaller things here and there, like an unpaid water lien for a couple of hundred bucks or an extra signature needed from a seller if it's an estate. You should not buy a property unless you have had a title company do their search to ensure marketable title. That is why I also recommend getting title insurance. If you have a lender, they require a lender's title policy, but you should also get an owner's title policy, which we will go over in the next section.

## 95. Should I Buy Owner's Title Insurance?

When you buy a house with a loan, there are two types of title insurance. Your lender has a lender's title insurance policy to protect their interests, and there is also an option owner's title insurance policy to protect your interests. This one-time cost for the owner's policy helps to protect you in the event that there are any legal claims against the property that could affect the title.

Before you purchase the house, the title company will do a title search to make sure there is clean title and no current liens or legal claims against it. However, every now and then, undiscovered issues could arise from the history of the property, including unknown heirs, liens, pending lawsuits, forgery, legal judgments, fraud, and numerous other issues.

Having been a real estate investor and real estate broker for almost 10 years now, I have seen all of these issues. Owner's title insurance can help protect you in the event of these situations and gives you peace of mind when purchasing. I always recommend getting an owner's title insurance policy. I would say about 90 percent of the buyers get one.

They range in price from about 1K to upwards of 4K, depending on the price of the house. If the seller you are buying from has owned the home for less than 10 years and purchased an owner's title policy when they moved in, you can ask the title company for a re-issue rate on the policy. That would give you a significant discount on your owner's policy. Most title companies will check on this for you as a service.

## 96. What Does Homeowners' Insurance Cover?

If you finance your property, your lender will require that you have homeowner's insurance. There are different types of policies, like any insurance, but they generally cover things like fire, theft, frozen pipes, damage from thunderstorms, or injuries on your property. For more extreme areas, you will need to get additional earthquake and flood insurance since those are not covered in general homeowner's insurance.

Once your property is paid off or if you paid cash for the property, you technically don't need to buy homeowner's insurance, but I would highly recommend that you do. A house is a large asset, so if something disastrous happens, you want to be protected. Having worked in the real estate industry for the last 10 years, I hear about home insurance claims all the time. I can't imagine a good reason not to get this type of insurance. Be sure to shop around for the best rates and policies.

# SECTION 9

---

# After You Buy

## 97. What Part Of Buying A Home Is Tax Deductible?

I am not a CPA, so I am not giving you tax advice. That being said, one of the best parts of real estate is how many things you can deduct. When you do your taxes, you will also be giving your CPA your closing statement to make it easier. The main items you can deduct include any prepaid mortgage points, the interest paid on your mortgage, private mortgage insurance (PMI) if you have it, and the state and property taxes on your home.

Other tax breaks that you would need to verify with your CPA include energy-efficient upgrades for things like solar panels, home office deduction if you work from home, and interest on a home equity line of credit if it is used to improve your property. The best strategy is to keep copies of everything on paper and back it up online. Also, you should familiarize yourself online with different tax breaks and deductions before you send everything over to your CPA.

## 98. What Are The Biggest Expenses For First-Time Home Buyers?

Once you move into your first home, you should always have a reserve fund for unexpected expenses – especially if you buy a house. A townhome and condo generally need significantly fewer repairs, but you should always have a rainy-day fund. In addition to all the new furniture, painting, and other updates you might be doing, you need to be prepared for significant expenses, such as HVAC, plumbing, electrical, roof issues, and even landscaping.

Before buying the property, you should have a good idea of how old the roof and HVAC are, as those are usually the two most significant repairs. I would recommend making a list of future repairs that need to be done and start doing ballpark estimates of how much they will cost and how much you need to budget for them.

A quick online search on sites like HomeAdvisor and Angie's List can tell you exactly how much these repairs would be. I would add up all the repairs you think you'll need to make in the next five years. Once you have that total, you should add ten percent. This will be your rainy-day fund for updates, maintenance, and renovations.

## 99. Which Home Improvements Can I Get The Best Return On?

If you are buying a fixer upper and want to make sure you get the most value from your renovations, then this part is for you. The first and least expensive thing you should do is landscaping. It's amazing how different a house can appear with some simple landscaping improvement. You can talk to local garden centers who offer free design services or get some ideas online, such as new sod, a new walkway, and more.

In addition to landscaping, you should work on your curb appeal and consider new vinyl siding, painting, removing old awnings, and outdoor lighting. Next, you should consider fully renovating or at least updating the bathrooms.

After the bathrooms, you should tackle the kitchen and do updates such as appliances, backsplash, new light fixtures, or if you have the funds, a complete kitchen renovation. Bathrooms and kitchens are two of the most common things brought up when looking at houses.

Lastly, I think you should remodel or at least update your basement. A house with an unfinished basement is much tougher to sell. If you can make your downstairs area inviting, warm, and updated, it can add a ton of value.

Other things to consider include replacing windows, adding a deck or patio, or even doing an addition if it's a smaller house. Overall, though, I would focus on the curb appeal and landscaping first and foremost and then invest in your bathrooms, kitchen, and basement for the best ROI.

## 100. Is There Anything I Can Do To Eliminate Noise?

If you find yourself looking at a property or you've already purchased a property that happens to be noisy, then there are several ways to lower the noise. There is literally an entire industry around soundproofing homes, studios, and more. For starters, you can add insulation and redo your drywall with soundproof drywall, such as Quietrock and others. That will have a significant impact on noise.

Additionally, you can replace your windows with more soundproofing-efficient windows. Windows are generally more expensive so if you're looking for a budget-friendly option, you can weather-strip your windows and doors and fill in the gaps with an acoustical caulk sealant.

Another thing you can do is install a solid-core door as opposed to the common hollow-core doors. The more mass you have in your door, the less noise will come through.

In addition to those three ideas, there are countless others, including even soundproofing paint which can reduce sound by as much as 30%, tightening floorboards, soundproof underlayment for floors, putting in rugs, and many others. If you spent a weekend properly planning and strategizing, you could make your condo, townhouse, or single-family home much quieter.

## 101. What Is The Cost Of Maintaining A House?

The answer is, more than you think. I've touched on this already, but you should have at least three to six months' income in reserves. You will be paying for your mortgage as well as fees like utilities, cable/internet, and repairs and maintenance.

A good rule of thumb is, the older your property, the more you should budget and save. One thing you can do is buy a home warranty that will help you out with the cost of maintaining parts of the house. Overall, though, I would make sure you get a good home inspection and keep in mind the age of the big ticket items like the roof and

HVAC, and the cost of any updates you want to do.

# Ten Tips for Selling Your House

This book is all about what you should know when you buy a house. However, as an experienced real estate broker and real estate investor, I also want to tell you the ten things you must do if you want to get the top price when you go to sell your property. I've seen houses that get multiple offers above asking price, other properties that get offers under 100K asking price, and everything in between. If you want to sell quickly for a premium price, then follow these steps.

1. **Get a local real estate agent with excellent reviews.** What I'm really trying to say is, if you want to successfully sell your property, do not gamble by doing a for sale by owner or using your friend or family member who got their license yesterday. Use a local, full-time agent who comes recommended and has good reviews online.

2. **Professional photos.** We touched on this a little bit earlier, but make sure your agent gets professional photography done. If they are a full-time agent and come recommended, I would be shocked if they didn't hire a professional photographer, but every now and then, you might find one.

   Professional photography will make even the drabbest property look impressive. This will get the maximum number of people in the door. Professional photography usually only costs about $300, and your agent should willingly be able to cover that.

3. **Stage your property.** If you are living there, you can have a stager give you some tips. It should not be too hard. Mostly it

involves de-personalizing, de-cluttering, and adding some plants. Some people overlook this step, but our staged properties show much better and sell much faster than vacant homes. Vacant properties look cold, uninviting, and smaller than properties with furniture in them.

4. **Home inspection and repair.** Consider getting a home inspection done before you put it on the market and fixing up any necessary repairs. Some sellers will get an inspection done before they list the property so that they can fix any big or small issues. This is a proactive strategy that works well. The one downside to this is, if you find anything major in the report, you will have to disclose it to the future buyer.

5. **Do not do a FSBO.** I know that I have mentioned this earlier, but I don't care if you live in the hottest neighborhood of all time where every house gets multiple offers. FSBO properties sit on the market longer, and many buyers ignore FSBOs because they are almost always overpriced. Sometimes the buyers don't even know they exist. Get the property

listed properly with a local agent so you can get the proper exposure and the highest price.

6. **Price it right.** Do not try to get significantly over the comps. It's better to generate a lot of interest. Just because one house in your neighborhood sold for one million dollars does not mean your home will get that price. Your agent should advise you on a realistic and correct price. If you shoot for the moon with your price, the house will often sit on the market, and you will have to go through a series of price chops. People will start to wonder what's wrong with the house and send you lowball offers.

7. **Make your house accessible.** This sounds obvious, but you should make it as easy as possible to view the property. I've seen sellers that only allow showings at very specific times, such as between 6 and 9 p.m. on Tuesdays, and it only works to their detriment. Be flexible. I've had buyers simply skip houses entirely because they were not able to see it at a particular time and day.

8. **Secure valuables.** You should not have expensive watches, sports memorabilia, or other things lying around your property. If you have a security camera on them, that's okay, but you never know what can happen. I've received calls from the sheriff before asking about a missing watch and other things. Make sure to keep everything in a safe or tucked away. While it's unusual for this type of thing to happen, you need to be prepared.

9. **Keep up landscaping, keep lights on as much as possible, and control the temperature.** In real estate, first impressions are critical. Make sure your place has a weekly or bi-weekly landscaper, the lights are always on, and the temperature is good. You can put the lights on a timer if you are more comfortable with that.

There is nothing like walking up to a nice landscaped yard into a bright open house at a cool, relaxing temperature. It leaves a great impression and can make any house stand out. Moreover, it does not cost that much. Dark houses turn people off. You would be surprised how many people don't even test the lighting.

10. **Spring is the best time to sell.** The last tip is that spring is the best time to sell according to Zillow's research – and as common sense dictates. Try to list your property between March and May if you want to have the highest number of buyers and get the highest price. Houses have historically sold fastest during these time periods. It's not the end of the world if you have to sell during another time of year, but if you can, you should shoot for the spring.

# BONUS 2

# House-Buying Hacks

In this section, I have included some house-buying hacks that most buyers do not think of and, in some cases, are not aware of.

1. **Put basement suites on Airbnb.** If you buy a house in an area close to the city, you should consider having an Airbnb suite in your property. Ideally, you could buy a house with a basement suite that you can turn into a cash cow. The key to this is that you might need to renovate the basement or Airbnb suite, and you need to make sure you buy close to the restaurants and shops.

   Even if you don't want to rent out the basement, you can consider putting your place on Airbnb when you go out of town for vacation. Always check the rules and regulations for your area, but in most cases, as long as there is no condo or HOA association, you should be good.

2. **Buy near a Whole Foods**. If you want your property to appreciate in value, you should consider buying a house within close proximity of a Whole Foods. According to the real estate book *Zillow Talk*, if you buy within a mile of a Whole Foods or Trader Joe's, your property value has a significantly increased likelihood to appreciate in value.

These large companies spend millions of dollars on researching the next up-and-coming neighborhoods, so I would rely on their research when buying your first house.

3. **Buy a 4-unit property with FHA**. In case you didn't know, you can buy a multiunit property as your first purchase for as little as 3.5% down with an FHA loan. This means you could live in one of the units and rent the other three units out.

Theoretically, if you found the right property, you could live for free and save up for another year or two before repeating the process on another apartment building with a larger conventional down payment. Most people overlook multi units for their first property. However, if you buy a building that does not need a ton of work, this is a great way to build equity.

4. **Make offers on houses that have a contract on them.** One overlooked way of finding great deals is staying in touch with homes that are already under contract. I am not sure of the exact numbers, but if I were to guess, somewhere in the ballpark of 10% of properties fall out of contract for various reasons.

If you contact the agent, they will usually tell you whether the contract looks shaky or not and you can line up to be the next purchaser. You can write a backup offer, or in many cases, the agent will just let you and your agent know first if anything happens with the first offer.

5. **Pay attention to those "we buy houses" signs you see everywhere.** If you live in a metropolitan area, you have probably seen those handwritten "we buy houses" signs on the side of the road and elsewhere. What exactly are they? Are they legitimate? Those signs you see are usually newer real estate investors looking for leads. They put a lot of these signs up, hoping that motivated sellers will call them looking for a cash buyer instead of listing their property on the market.

You can compile a list of these signs and tell them to let you know if they come across any good deals. Many times, the people that put up bandit signs, as they are called, will sell the rights of a deal to another investor. They are called wholesalers and provide leads to investors or, if you are savvy enough, first-time home buyers like yourself. If you have 10 of these people sending you any deals they come across, then chances are you could see some good off-market deals.

6. **Ask for a reissue rate.** If you want to save an easy $500 or so dollars on your next purchase, ask the seller for a copy of their

owner's title policy so that you can get a re-issue rate.

Many title companies should automatically do this for you, but if the owner has lived there less than 10 years and bought an owner's title policy, then you could get a big discount on your closing costs. A seller will not object to this and it is a significant saving.

7. **Look up estate sales.** Sometimes the best deals can be found at estate sales. I'm not talking about furniture and old CDs. If you regularly look up the estate sales on Craigslist and other areas in your neighborhood, you can ask the person there if they are selling the property.

Many times, the representative will want to liquidate the estate with the least hassle possible. If you make them a fair offer and don't ask for any repairs to be done, you can get a great deal. In every market, there are estate sales that never hit the MLS because they sell quickly to an as-is buyer, and they usually get a great price.

8. **Look at houses with bad pictures.** If the property meets a lot of your criteria but has terrible pictures, then I would still recommend looking at it. Bad pictures mean the agent and seller are not correctly marketing the house, and there will be significantly fewer buyers looking at it.

Fewer buyers mean more opportunity for you. You could end up getting a great deal since there is not as much competition. More times than not, seeing a property online is very different from viewing it in person, so don't write off properties that are poorly marketed.

9. **Look at properties with mold and structural issues.** If you come from a background in construction, I would recommend looking at properties that have mold and structural problems. 99% of the buyers out there are completely turned off by properties like this, even if it's a small amount of mold or other issues.

More times than not, though, the actual cost of fixing the mold or structural issue is significantly less than people think. If you have experience with these types of repairs, just factor them into your offer price and then go much lower.

There are not a lot of buyers for these types of houses, so you can be very aggressive in your offer price. I used to know one investor who would specifically look at the MLS for the keywords "mold, water issues," and other similar words since he knew exactly how to remediate the issue. FYI: this is only for those that have a background in construction.

**10. Buy in a gayborhood.** Another interesting note from Zillow's book *Zillow Talk* is that they found that "home prices in historically gay neighborhoods have steadily" outperformed other neighborhoods. That basically means, if you want your property to appreciate, you should look towards "gay" neighborhoods.

# Top Mistakes First-Time Home Buyers Make

In this section, we go over the top 10 mistakes I see first-time home buyers make.

1. **Emptying your savings to make the deal work**. If you are pinching every last penny to make the deal work, I would advise you to be very careful. The thing with a significant investment like real estate is that there are always unexpected costs or repairs on the house as well as sudden life changes. When buying a home, I highly recommend that you have a safety reserve fund of at least three to six months of income.

2. **Getting only one quote for a mortgage.** When getting a mortgage, or any service for that matter, you should always have at least an idea of what the closest competitors are offering. I would recommend getting three estimates and then choosing the best. It does not necessarily have to be the cheapest option, but you want to get a good idea of the mortgages available and how different companies work.

3. **Buying something large before closing happens**. One of the dumbest mistakes I have seen people make (no offense!) is making a massive purchase before closing or switching jobs. For the 30 days or so that you are under contract before you close, make sure not to do anything that would affect your ability to qualify for a loan. Your lender should tell you this as well, but hold off on switching jobs until after you close on the house. And don't buy that brand-new car until after you move in.

4. **Buying the first house they see instead of looking at 100**. Some buyers are motivated to move ASAP and don't have six

months to look at homes or anything. That is fine, but I would recommend that you try to see at least 100 houses, whether it's browsing online or ideally at open houses.

Spend a couple of weekends visiting properties at open houses so you can get an idea of living there instead of just looking at pictures. It will be very different. As investors, we like to look at 100 deals before choosing one or two. I would take the same approach with choosing your primary residence. You don't need to visit 100 homes personally, but you should see at least 10-25 in person just to get an idea and then do a ton of browsing online.

5. **Lowballing every offer to get a "steal of a deal."** Many first-time home buyers get the idea that they can lowball every offer and that the seller will meet them in the middle between their offer price and the sales price. I very rarely see the seller drop their price significantly.

When I do, it's for properties that either need a lot of work, have been sitting on the market for a while, or have a super motivated seller who needs to get out ASAP. Your agent should recommend an aggressive price for any property, but that does not mean lowballing every house is a viable strategy.

6. **Trying to buy a house without an agent.** Trying to buy a house without an agent is not a great idea. I've said this before, even the most mediocre agent is better than you trying to go it alone. There are certain ways of doing a real estate transaction that someone who is not an agent will not understand.

I can guarantee you will make some rookie mistakes if you try to do it alone. From my own experience, it's always the people who think they don't need an agent that probably need a whole team of agents advising them. Also, any time a listing agent sees an unrepresented buyer, it's like there is blood in the water and they know the seller is in for a much better deal.

7. **Underestimating renovation costs.** If you are buying a fixer upper as your first property, you are probably adding up the total

costs of the renovations. What I see happen too often with new home buyers, as well as new investors, is that they completely underestimate the time and cost involved.

While fixer-uppers can be a great idea, just make sure you've done your research on how much the repairs will cost. You can research online, ask your agent, get a contractor estimate. And whatever repair number you come up with, make sure to add 10%, or 15% if it's a larger project.

8. **Not researching the neighborhood.** Always make sure you get a good idea of the area before buying. While that sounds obvious, I've seen so many instances where people have not done proper research and end up having to sell their place after a year for a loss because they can't stand the neighborhood.

Usually, it is because of commute time, amenities, and distance from friends and family. Make sure you read every possible article about the area you are thinking of moving to. You can also hang out there at events, spend a couple of days in an Airbnb, drive through the neighborhood at night, and anything else you can think of.

9. **Not considering resale value.** When buying a house, you may plan on living there for the next 30 years, and reselling the property in the next five to 10 years is not in the plans. That being said, while I know you are looking for the "perfect house," you should also keep in mind resale value.

That means, be careful if you find the perfect house in the middle of nowhere. It can be tempting to buy an amazing house far outside the core of the city since your money can go so much further. Just be careful and plan on the property not appreciating very much – if at all. I can tell you story after story of people buying "a palace in nowhere-land," only to see their property is worth the same or even less 10 years later. Location is everything in real estate.

10. **Buying a house with a cousin who is your agent.** Everybody knows someone who is a real estate agent these days. I would

recommend not working with a friend or family member if they just got their license. Now, if they are a full-time real estate agent, that is a different scenario, and you can work with them. However, there are things that new real estate agents will not be aware of that an experienced agent will know how to do. Make sure to use a full-time professional for every aspect of your home-buying process.

# Conclusion

Thanks again for taking the time to read this guide. By finishing this book, you now have everything you need to know about the home-buying process. If you follow the ideas and tips in this book, you will be ahead of the competition and be a savvier buyer than the majority of the buyers out there. I wrote this book because I wanted to share almost 10 years of experience with the actual home-buying process without all the nonsense you might hear on the news or from people that are not in the business every day.

If you have any questions or are looking at buying a house in DC, VA, or MD areas, then contact me at info@actionhomebuyers.com. My team can assist you. We also have partners nationwide, so if you are looking for assistance buying property anywhere, just email us and we can help you.

I hope that you have great success in your home-buying process. Drop me a note when you buy your first house and let me know how this book helped you out.

Also, I appreciate any type of feedback. If you got value from my book, I would appreciate you leaving a review on Amazon so that I can get my message out there even more.

Thanks again!

Jeff Leighton

# About The Author

Jeff Leighton is a real estate broker, real estate investor, and bestselling Amazon Author. He has been mentored by some of the top real estate investors in the US and continues to buy and sell real estate to this day.

# Want More Info?

Go to www.Jeff-Leighton.com for helpful videos, free resources, downloads, and much, much more.

## Other Books By The Author

Available on Amazon

## Follow Jeff Leighton

Instagram.com/J_Late12
YouTube.com/JeffLeighton1
Facebook.com/JeffLeighton5

Made in the USA
Middletown, DE
20 May 2021